First Edition
11 10 09 08 07      5 4 3 2 1

Published by
Gibbs Smith, Publisher
P.O. Box 667
Layton, Utah 84041

Orders: 1.800.835.4993
www.gibbs-smith.com

Created By: **Jeanette R. Lynton**

Executive Director: **Kristine Widtfeldt**

Creative Manager: **Kristy McDonnell**

Art Director: **Eric Clegg**

Graphic Designer: **John Youngberg**

Project Manager: **Stacy San Juan**

Writers: **Tori Bahoravitch, JoAnn Jolley,**
   **Stephanie Olsen**

Copy Editor: **Ben Williamson**

Production Editors: **Adam Cazier,**
   **Rose Hales, Katelyn Ryskamp**

Photographer: **Skylar Nielsen**

Printed in China

Thank you to all the talented stamp artists who helped make these fabulous layouts come to life.

For information about the products used in these layouts, please contact an Independant Close To My Heart Consultant by calling **888-655-6552,** or visit **www.closetomyheart.com**.

Library of Congress Cataloging-in-Publication Data
Library of Congress Control Number:  2007924605
ISBN 13: 978-1-4236-0312-2
ISBN 10: 1-4236-0312-5

# Imagine

## FUN, FABULOUS LAYOUTS FOR EVERY SCRAPBOOKER

**Gibbs Smith, Publisher**

TO ENRICH AND INSPIRE HUMANKIND

*Salt Lake City* | *Charleston* | *Santa Fe* | *Santa Barbara*

## Dear Friends:

When did your love of scrapbooking begin? The day you got married? That unforgettable vacation to Europe? Or perhaps when your first child was born?

For me, my passion for scrapbooking ignited when I was a young girl equipped with an instamatic camera and a world of creative ideas. I couldn't wait to capture my memories of friends and family and preserve them in beautiful layouts I treasure to this day.

While I know that many share my passion for scrapbooking, through the years scores of people have told me they struggle to get the design just right. What sizes should photos be? How do I keep the proportions right? Where should I put my title? How do I balance all the elements in a layout? Do I really need journaling?

As a designer and artist for more than 20 years, I have developed hundreds of unique patterns that answer these questions—beautifully! My life's work has been developing a philosophy of scrapbooking, the products to support it, and a line of books to teach the world how to make scrapbooking faster, simpler, and easier. What began with the *Reflections Scrapbook Program*™ in the mid-nineties evolved into *Cherish*™, which underwent many printings in its first year of publication.

With that history, I'm thrilled to bring you my latest creation—*Imagine*™, designed to help you set your imagination free. With this foolproof guide, you can create the pages of your dreams and enjoy the process, too. Step-by-step instructions, my trademark blueprints, and easy-to-follow cutting diagrams have done all the work for you. Select your papers, add your favorite photos, and let your imagination do the rest!

Make it from your heart,

*Jeanette*

## JEANETTE R. LYNTON

Since the 1970s, Jeanette has enjoyed a passion for preserving treasured memories, and early in life began creating exclusive stamps and sharing her scrapbooking knowledge. Today, Close To My Heart, the company Jeanette founded, is a leader in the scrapbooking and stamping industry.

Always at the forefront of innovation and creativity, Jeanette's new products have included the world's first true 12" × 12" scrapbooking format; a series of instructional programs offering simple guidelines for dynamic scrapbook layouts and homemade cards; scrapbooking kits featuring pre-printed layouts; and My Acrylix® clear decorative stamps and blocks that allow for perfect stamp placement.

Jeanette's artistic eye and "let me show you how" approach have made scrapbooking faster, simpler, and easier than ever before, while continuing to enhance the art of preserving memories and celebrating relationships.

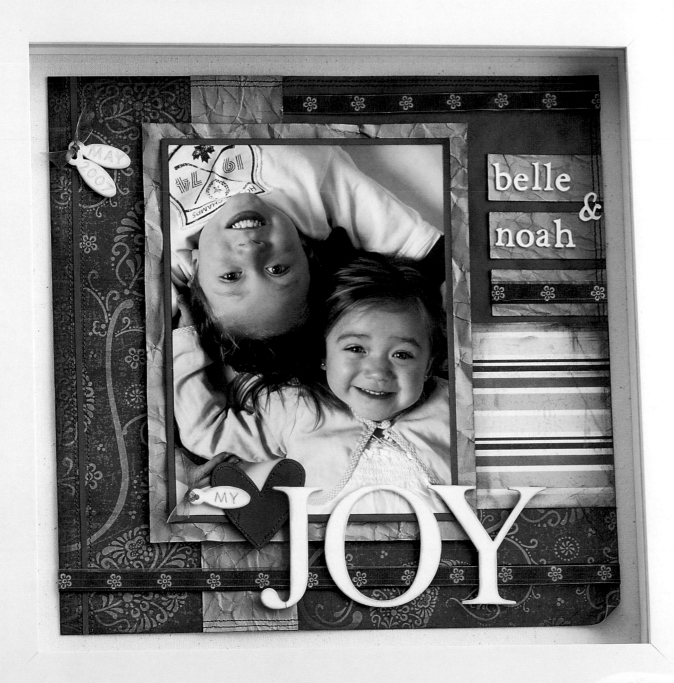

# Imagine the Possibilities

Close your eyes for a moment. Go ahead, trust me. Envision yourself as a child, outside on a summer morning. The air smells of cut grass. The sun is warm on your cheeks. Today is so full of possibilities. You want to sing at the top of your lungs. You feel perfectly free.

That's the spirit of *Imagine*™—a book designed with all the right ingredients to deliver a recipe for perfect creative freedom. To make the most of this book, consider these helpful steps:

1. Always start with photos. They are the centerpiece of your layout and the heart of the story it will tell. Work with photos from a single event, day, or theme for simplicity.

2. Use the Quick Reference to select a layout. This guide makes it easy to find a layout that matches the quantity and orientation of your chosen photos.

3. Pick your papers. Choose papers that complement your photos, pulling prominent colors from clothing, scenery, or other elements in the photos. Ensure you choose papers required for the layout.

4. Choose a technique. Before you begin cutting and assembly, select a technique that supports the look you're going for—a camping layout may look great with rugged distressing, but that Easter layout calls for delicate chalking or sponging. Select a single technique per layout to keep the artwork focused on your photos.

5. Build it! Now comes the fun—follow the instructions to transform your papers into beautiful artwork faster, simpler, and easier!

6. Add photos, title, and journaling. Once the construction is complete, add photos (matted where appropriate). Always add a title to give your layout a visual anchor, and journaling to preserve the specifics. Now, stand back and admire!

7. Remember the finishing touches. Is your layout missing something? Maybe not. But if it is, this is the step where you may wish to accessorize your layout with coordinating embellishments—just enough to complete the look, not overwhelm it.

## TRANSFORM IT WITH TECHNIQUE

A new technique can add pizzazz to any layout—and trying something new can be fun, too! *Imagine* includes a variety of techniques, from elementary to sophisticated, so you can experiment all you want. The more complex techniques are showcased with in-depth photos and instructions, while simpler techniques are detailed at the back of the book.

## TELL YOUR STORY

The heart of your layout is the story behind it—and we want the details! Capture the funny comments, the names and places, the important achievements, even notes on the weather. Years from now, you'll forget these gems, but your journaling will remember. Each layout includes title and journaling suggestions that are flexible; adjust them to work for you, but never eliminate them!

We really enjoy the
.tdoors. Each year when
.e leaves begin to chang
color we try and take a
weekend trip to the
mountains. This
particular trip was t
Keystone, Colorado.
was absolutely gorgeo

## TEAR IT UP!

Many of my favorite layouts in *Imagine* involve paper tearing, which I love because it adds life and personality. For best results, tear no more than ½" off the original, trimmed piece—the cutting diagrams and instructions will guide you, and include dimensions for the piece both before and after tearing. For dramatically different effects, consider:

• **Small tears**—give your edges a more refined, deckled look by tearing paper away in smaller, more delicate strokes, using very little of your ½" "tearing margin."

• **Large tears**—create rugged peaks and valleys by using the entire ½" "tearing margin" of your paper. Always use cardstock with a white core to highlight your tear.

• **Precise tears**—if you want to ensure your tear follows a precise line, I suggest you "draw" your tear line using water and a fine paintbrush. Allowing the water to absorb briefly into the paper will soften the fibers and ensure a perfect tear every time.

• **No tear at all**—prefer a perfectly clean, smooth edge? Simply trim the ½" "tear margin" completely off with your paper trimmer and continue the cutting and assembly instructions as outlined.

# My Favorite Things

After decades of scrapbooking, I'll admit that I love it all! All the papers, all the embellishments, all the tools, everything! But there are a few essential products I'd be lost without. You'll see loving and lavish use of my "favorite things" on the pages of *Imagine*™, but I can't resist the chance to tell you why these three basics are must-haves for your special layouts.

### ADORE THE CORE

Your mother told you "it's what's inside that counts." And that is true, particularly when it comes to cardstock! Whether you love smooth cardstock or the totally textured varieties, cardstock simply must have a white core. Here's why you "get more with the core":

• Sand, scissor, dry-emboss, or otherwise distress white-core cardstock to let that white core peek through for a million different looks. Watch as your cardstock is transformed into beadboard or a watercolor canvas or adds a dimensional design that pops into view.

• Tear white-core cardstock for dramatic borders and color contrast without adding more paper to your project.

### SEE CLEARLY NOW

How did we ever stamp with wood-and-rubber stamps? Clear stamps haven't just changed the way I scrapbook, they have revolutionized the entire market. If you haven't discovered them yet, you'll love the incredible precision, easy storage, and versatility these stamps deliver.

### INSPIRE WITH INK

You don't have to be a stamper to love ink pads. In fact, you'll find many of the techniques in *Imagine* use stamp pads in innovative ways. Try stippling with ink for a spiky or impressionistic effect. Sponge on ink for soft edges and a gentle kiss of color. Apply ink with a waterbrush for a painted look. Or try one of my favorite techniques—

direct-to-paper "swiping." Simply "swipe" the edge of your paper across the pad's surface for a distressed look. Everyone should own black and brown hues just for this hot, versatile technique!

My favorite inks are dye-based for easy blending, layering, and use in a variety of crafting projects. Choose a quality brand in a sealed case that stores ink upside down. This type of packaging will prevent ink from drying out and will keep color close to the surface when you're ready to use it. And if you love perfect color matching—and who doesn't?— make sure to choose a brand of stamp pads with a coordinating line of color papers. That way, your projects will always have spot-on color!

# Quick Reference

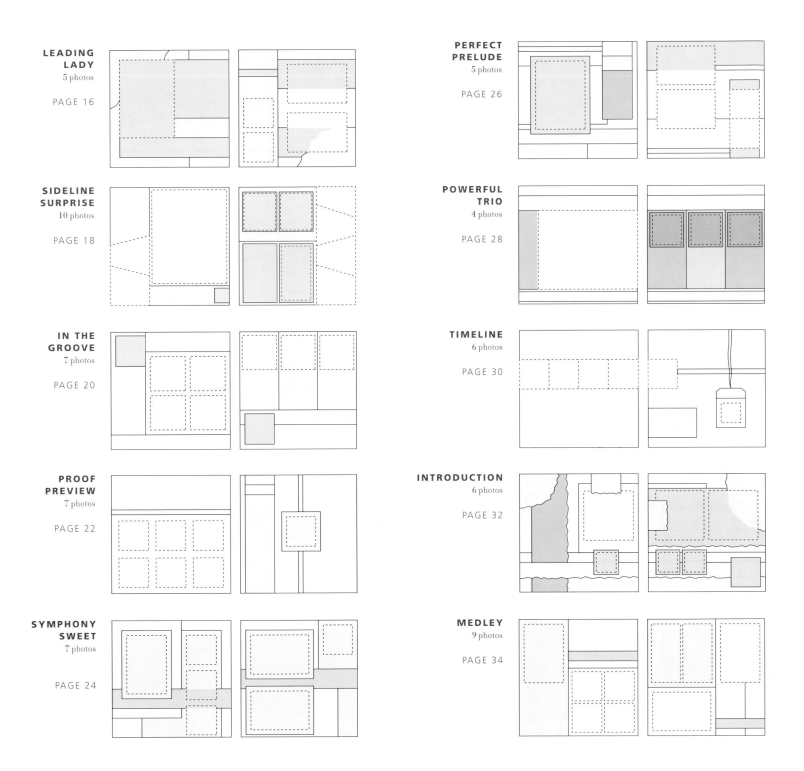

**LEADING LADY**
5 photos

PAGE 16

**SIDELINE SURPRISE**
10 photos

PAGE 18

**IN THE GROOVE**
7 photos

PAGE 20

**PROOF PREVIEW**
7 photos

PAGE 22

**SYMPHONY SWEET**
7 photos

PAGE 24

**PERFECT PRELUDE**
5 photos

PAGE 26

**POWERFUL TRIO**
4 photos

PAGE 28

**TIMELINE**
6 photos

PAGE 30

**INTRODUCTION**
6 photos

PAGE 32

**MEDLEY**
9 photos

PAGE 34

**SERENADE**
6 photos

PAGE 36

**JAZZY COMBINATION**
6 photos

PAGE 38

**ENSEMBLE PIECE**
6 photos

PAGE 40

**CONCERTO**
6 photos

PAGE 42

**THREE-PART HARMONY**
6 photos

PAGE 44

**MINUET**
7 photos

PAGE 46

**DYNAMIC DUO**
7 photos

PAGE 48

**MONOLOGUE**
5 photos

PAGE 52

**EVERYTHING IN ITS PLACE**
10 photos

PAGE 54

**CONCLUSION COMBO**
12 photos

PAGE 56

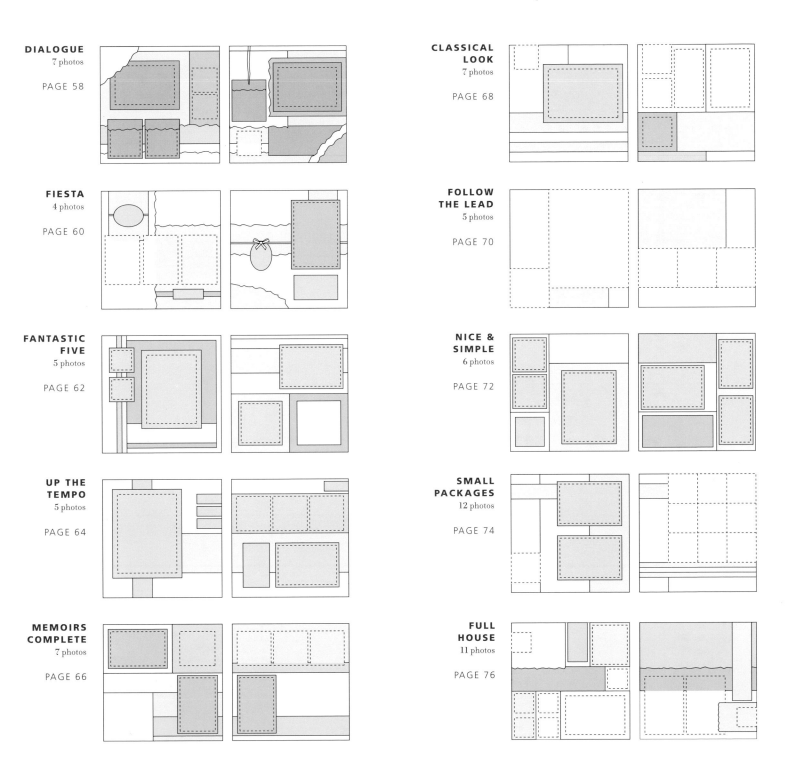

**DIALOGUE**
7 photos

PAGE 58

**FIESTA**
4 photos

PAGE 60

**FANTASTIC FIVE**
5 photos

PAGE 62

**UP THE TEMPO**
5 photos

PAGE 64

**MEMOIRS COMPLETE**
7 photos

PAGE 66

**CLASSICAL LOOK**
7 photos

PAGE 68

**FOLLOW THE LEAD**
5 photos

PAGE 70

**NICE & SIMPLE**
6 photos

PAGE 72

**SMALL PACKAGES**
12 photos

PAGE 74

**FULL HOUSE**
11 photos

PAGE 76

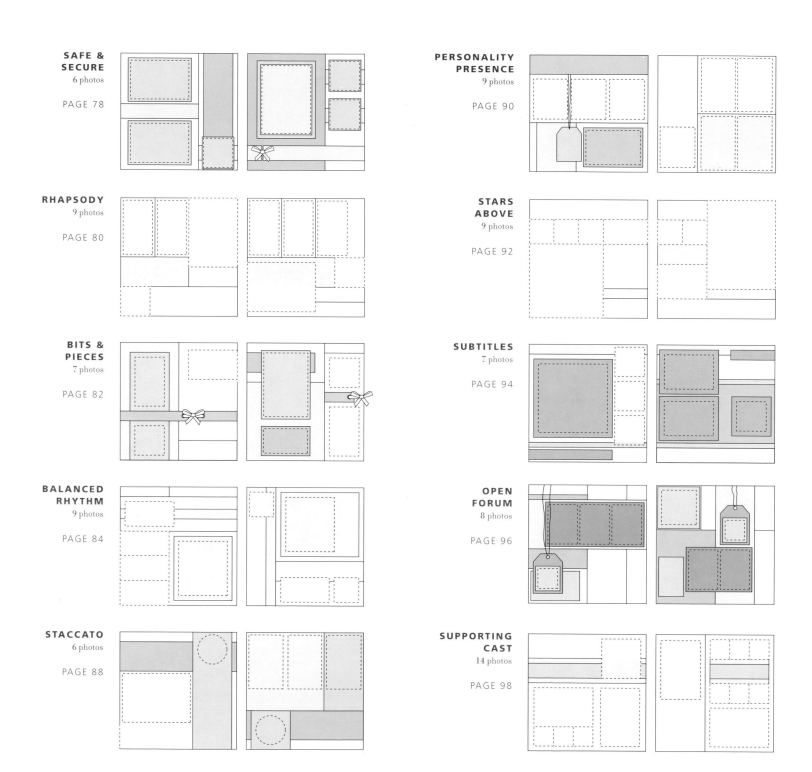

**SAFE & SECURE**
6 photos

PAGE 78

**RHAPSODY**
9 photos

PAGE 80

**BITS & PIECES**
7 photos

PAGE 82

**BALANCED RHYTHM**
9 photos

PAGE 84

**STACCATO**
6 photos

PAGE 88

**PERSONALITY PRESENCE**
9 photos

PAGE 90

**STARS ABOVE**
9 photos

PAGE 92

**SUBTITLES**
7 photos

PAGE 94

**OPEN FORUM**
8 photos

PAGE 96

**SUPPORTING CAST**
14 photos

PAGE 98

# Quick Reference

**THUMBNAILS**
16 photos

PAGE 100

**DOUBLE TAKE**
5 photos

PAGE 102

**CREATIVE TEAM**
7 photos

PAGE 104

**ROLE PLAY**
7 photos

PAGE 106

**GRAND FINALE**
4 photos

PAGE 108

**UNDERSTUDY**
7 photos

PAGE 110

**SWING RHYTHM**
7 photos

PAGE 112

**SHADOW**
4 photos

PAGE 114

**OVERTURE**
9 photos

PAGE 116

**SALSA**
6 photos

PAGE 118

Nurture

# Leading Lady

### Layout Materials

12" × 12" Base Cardstock (2)
12" × 12" Cardstock (2)
12" × 12" B&T Paper (2)

### Left Page Dimensions

A  6" × 6" (torn diagonally)
B  12" × 4"
C  10" × 11"
D  2" × 5½"

### Right Page Dimensions

E  12" × 4"
F  ¾" × 4"
G  10" × 8"
H  6" × 6" (torn diagonally)
I  4" × 8"

### Photo Suggestions

1  8" × 5½"
2  3" × 3" (2)
3  4" × 6" (2)

### Suggested Title/Journaling

1  5½" × 5"

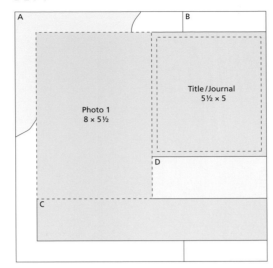

Photo 1
8 × 5½

Title/Journal
5½ × 5

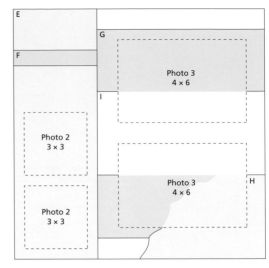

Photo 3
4 × 6

Photo 2
3 × 3

Photo 3
4 × 6

Photo 2
3 × 3

**1** Decoratively tear or cut piece A (H) in half diagonally as shown in the cutting diagrams.

**2** Using one 12" × 12" cardstock as your base, attach piece A to the top left corner of the page, keeping the edges flush.

**3** Attach piece B to the right side of the page, keeping the right edges flush.

**4** Attach piece C to the right side of the page, placing it 1" from the top, keeping the right edges flush.

**5** Attach piece D to the right side of the page, placing it 3" from the bottom, keeping the right edges flush.

**6** Attach the specified photo (photo 1) to the appropriate area.

**1** Decoratively tear or cut piece H (A) in half diagonally as shown in the cutting diagrams.

**2** Using one 12" × 12" cardstock as your base, attach piece E to the left side of the page, keeping the edges flush.

**3** Attach piece F to piece E, placing it 2" from the top of the page, keeping the left edges flush.

**4** Attach piece G to the right side of the page, placing it 1" from the top edge, keeping the right edges flush.

**5** Attach piece H to the bottom right corner of the page, keeping the edges flush.

**6** Attach piece I 3" from the top of piece G overlapping piece H, keeping the right edges flush.

**7** Attach the specified photos (photos 2-3) to the appropriate areas.

### JEANETTE'S TIP

Words included in various ways—through a title, accents, facts, or subtle designs— can stand alone or help tell your story.

**Easy Accents with Precut Embellishments.**
*For full Recipe and Technique see index pg. 120*

## Cutting Instructions

**B&T Paper**

| I |
|---|
| 4 × 8 |

| B |
|---|
| 12 × 4 |

SCRAP

**B&T Paper**

| A |
|---|
| 6 × 6 |

| H |

| E |
|---|
| 12 × 4 |

| D |
|---|
| 2 × 5½ |

SCRAP

**Cardstock***

| C |
|---|
| 10 × 11 |

| F ¾ × 4 |

SCRAP

**Cardstock***

| G |
|---|
| 10 × 8 |

SCRAP

*Identical papers

17

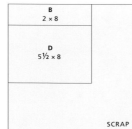

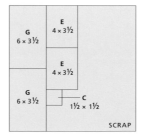

## Cutting Instructions

**B&T Paper**

| | |
|---|---|
| A<br>6½ × 4 | F<br>6½ × 8 |
| SCRAP | |

**B&T Paper**

| |
|---|
| B<br>2 × 8 |
| D<br>5½ × 8 |
| SCRAP |

**Cardstock**

| | |
|---|---|
| G<br>6 × 3½ | E<br>4 × 3½ |
| | E<br>4 × 3½ |
| G<br>6 × 3½ | C<br>1½ × 1½ |
| | SCRAP |

# Sideline Surprise

*Layout Materials*

12" × 12" Base
Cardstock (2)

12" × 12"
Cardstock (1)

12" × 12" B&T
Paper (2)

*Left Page
Dimensions*

A  6½" × 4"
B  2" × 8"
C  1½" × 1½"

*Right Page
Dimensions*

D  5½" × 8"
E  4" × 3½" (2)
F  6½" × 8"
G  6" × 3½" (2)

*Photo
Suggestions*

1  9½" × 7½"
2  4" × 4" (5)
   cut on angles
3  3" × 4" cut
   on angle
4  3½" × 3" (2)
5  5½" × 3"

*Suggested Title*

1  1" × 8"

*Suggested
Journaling*

1  5½" × 3"

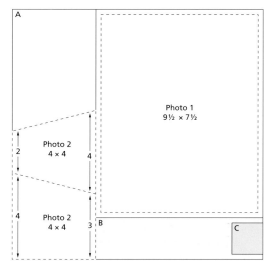

Photo 1
9½ × 7½

Photo 2
4 × 4

Photo 2
4 × 4

A
2
4
4
4
3
B
C

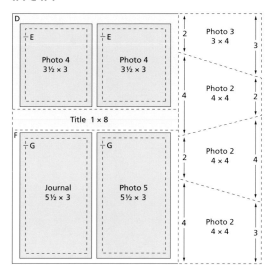

Photo 4
3½ × 3

Photo 4
3½ × 3

Title  1 × 8

Journal
5½ × 3

Photo 5
5½ × 3

Photo 3
3 × 4

Photo 2
4 × 4

Photo 2
4 × 4

Photo 2
4 × 4

D
E  E
F
G  G

**LEFT**

1  Using one 12" × 12" cardstock as your base, attach piece A to the top left corner of the page, keeping the edges flush.

2  Attach piece B to the bottom right corner of the page, keeping the edges flush.

3  Attach piece C to the bottom right corner of the page, placing it ¼" from the bottom edge, keeping the right edges flush.

4  Attach the specified photo (photo 1) to the appropriate area, centering it on the mat.

5  Arrange the specified photos (photos 2) down the left side of the page below piece A. Plan the cuts and angles that will best emphasize your photos. Cut one photo first and then use the angle to cut the second photo accordingly. Attach to the appropriate areas.

**RIGHT**

1  Using one 12" × 12" cardstock as your base, attach piece D to the top left corner of the page, keeping the edges flush.

2  Attach the two pieces E to piece D, placing them ½" from the top, ⅜" from the left, and ¼" from each other.

3  Attach piece F to the bottom left corner of the page, keeping the edges flush.

4  Attach the two pieces G to piece F, placing them ¼" from the bottom, ⅜" from the left and ¼" from each other.

5  Arrange the specified photos (photos 2-3) down the right side of the page. Plan the cuts and angles that will best emphasize your photos. Cut one photo first and then use the angle to cut the next photo accordingly. Attach to the appropriate areas.

6  Attach the specified photos (photos 4-5) to the appropriate areas, centering them on the mats.

**Textured Cardstock with subtle color**

**STEP 1**  Ink a rubber brayer with a color that coordinates with your layout.

**STEP 2**  Roll brayer across white textured cardstock several times for consistent coverage.

**JEANETTE'S TIP**

Eyelets and stamps are a simple way to create your own customized background and texture paper.

*For full Recipe see index pg. 120*

# In the Groove

## Layout Materials

12" × 12" Base Cardstock (2)
12" × 12" Cardstock (1)
12" × 12" B&T Paper (3)

### Left Page Dimensions

A  10½" × 3½"
B  3" × 3"
C  8½" × 8½"

### Right Page Dimensions

D  8" × 4" (2)
E  8" × 4"
F  1½" × 12"
G  3" × 3"

## Photo Suggestions

1  3½" × 3½" (7)

## Suggested Title

1  1½" × 8"

## Suggested Journaling

1  3½" × 11½"
2  2" × 8"

**LEFT**

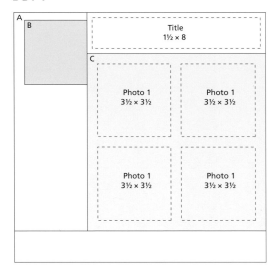

**RIGHT**

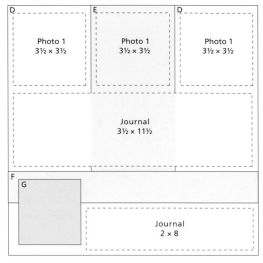

**1** Using one 12" × 12" cardstock as your base, attach piece A to the top left corner of the page, keeping the edges flush.

**2** Attach piece B to piece A, placing it ½" from the top and left edge of the page, keeping the right edges flush.

**3** Attach piece C to the right side of the page, placing it 2" from the top edge.

**4** Attach the specified photos (photos 1) to the appropriate areas.

**1** Using one 12" × 12" cardstock as your base, attach one piece D to the top left corner of the page, keeping the edges flush. Attach remaining piece D to the top right corner of the page, keeping the edges flush.

**2** Attach piece E between the two pieces D, keeping the edges flush.

**3** Attach piece F directly below pieces D and E, keeping the side edges flush.

**4** Attach piece G, placing it ½" from the bottom and left edges of the page.

**5** Attach the specified photos (photos 1) to the appropriate areas.

**JEANETTE'S TIP**

Differing fonts and varying word and letter sizes create an eye-catching effect on a title, journaling, and accents.

**Stamping on Twill Ribbon.** *For full Recipe and Technique see index pg. 120*

## Cutting Instructions

**B&T Paper**

| | | |
|---|---|---|
| **A** 10½ × 3½ | **D** 8 × 4 | **D** 8 × 4 |

SCRAP

**B&T Paper***

**F** 1½ × 12

**C** 8½ × 8½

SCRAP

**B&T Paper***

**E** 8 × 4

SCRAP

**Cardstock**

| **B** 3 × 3 | **G** 3 × 3 |
|---|---|

SCRAP

*Identical papers*

# Baby Boy

**Sixteen things about YOU**

16th grandchild (Dads side)

15 aunts and uncles to date

14 dimples on your cute behind

13th grandchild (Moms side)

11 pounds (8 ounces)

10 tiny fingers and toes

(at least) 9 diapers a day

8 goodnight kisses

7 good morning kisses

6 hours of sleep at night

(wish it was more)

5 square meals a day

4 months old

3 brothers who love you

2 beautiful brown eyes

1 perfect little boy

PREVIEW A SET OF PROOFS WITH THIS VERSATILE LAYOUT

................... *Cutting Instructions* ...................

**B&T Paper***

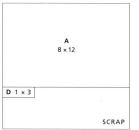

A
8 × 12

D 1 × 3

SCRAP

**B&T Paper***

E
12 × 6

SCRAP

**Cardstock**

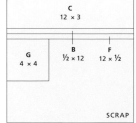

C
12 × 3

G
4 × 4

B
½ × 12

F
12 × ½

SCRAP

*Identical papers

# Proof Preview

## Layout Materials

12" × 12" Base
Cardstock (2)

12" × 12"
Cardstock (1)

12" × 12" B&T
Paper (2)

### Left Page Dimensions

A  8" × 12"
B  ½" × 12"

### Right Page Dimensions

C  12" × 3"
D  1" × 3"
E  12" × 6"
F  12" × ½"
G  4" × 4"

### Photo Suggestions

1  3" × 3" (7)

### Suggested Title

1  2½" × 8"

### Suggested Journaling

1  8" × 2½"

**LEFT**

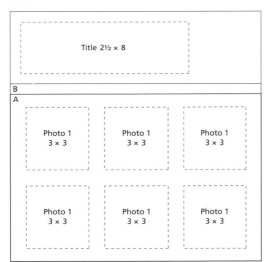

Title 2½ × 8

B
A

| Photo 1 3 × 3 | Photo 1 3 × 3 | Photo 1 3 × 3 |

| Photo 1 3 × 3 | Photo 1 3 × 3 | Photo 1 3 × 3 |

1  Using one 12" × 12" cardstock as your base, attach piece A to the bottom of the page, keeping the edges flush.

2  Attach piece B directly above piece A, keeping the edges flush.

3  Attach the specified photos (photos 1) to the appropriate areas.

**RIGHT**

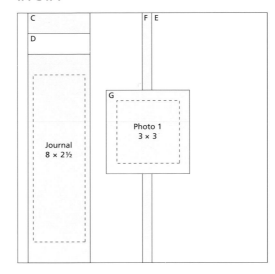

C
D
F  E

Journal 8 × 2½

G
Photo 1 3 × 3

1  Using one 12" × 12" cardstock as your base, attach piece C, placing it ½" from the left side of the page, keeping the top and bottom edges flush.

2  Attach piece D to piece C, placing it 1" from the top, keeping the side edges flush.

3  Attach piece E to the right side of the page, keeping the edges flush.

4  Attach piece F directly to the left of piece E, keeping the edges flush.

5  Attach piece G to the page, placing it 3¾" from the top and 4" from the right and left edges.

6  Attach the specified photo (photo 1) to the appropriate area, centering it on the mat.

## Wrapping Chipboard Frames

**STEP 1** Cut desired paper ½" larger than your frame. Attach frame to the back of the paper. Cut an X in the center of the frame from corner to corner. Cut off the tips of each triangle.

**STEP 2** Fold each side to the back, and glue. Round corners may need more cuts to create smooth edges.

**JEANETTE'S TIP**

Enhance the color sheme of any B&T paper by complementing it with a rich neutral tone and some distressing in the same color.

*For full Recipe see index pg. 120*

# Sweet Symphony

*Layout Materials*

12" × 12" Base Cardstock (2)
12" × 12" Cardstock (3)
12" × 12" B&T Paper (1)

*Left Page Dimensions*

A 11" × 8"
B 10" × 7"
C 2" × 12"
D 7" × 5"

*Right Page Dimensions*

E 12" × 4"
F 5" × 10"
G 2" × 12"
H 5" × 7" (2)

*Photo Suggestions*

1 6" × 4"
2 3" × 3" (4)
3 4" × 6" (2)

*Suggested Title*

1 1" × 6"

*Suggested Journaling*

1 1½" × 4"

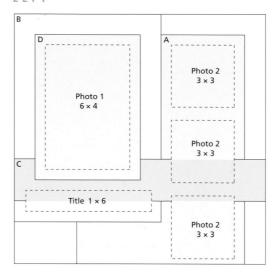

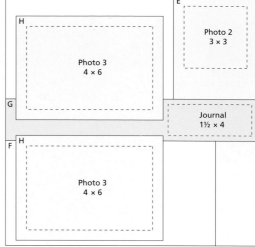

**LEFT**

1 Using one 12" × 12" cardstock as your base, attach piece A to the page, placing it 1" from the right edge, keeping the bottom edges flush.

2 Attach piece B to the top left corner of the page, keeping the edges flush.

3 Attach piece C across the page, placing it 3" from the bottom, keeping the side edges flush.

4 Attach piece D, placing it 1" from the top and left edges of the page.

5 Attach the specified photos (photos 1-2) to the appropriate areas, centering them on the mats.

**RIGHT**

1 Using one 12" × 12" cardstock as your base, attach piece E to the right side of the page, keeping the edges flush.

2 Attach piece F to the bottom left corner of the page, keeping the edges flush.

3 Attach piece G across the center of the page, placing it 5" from the top of the page, keeping the side edges flush.

4 Attach one piece H to the top of the page, placing it 1" from the top and ½" from the left edge. Attach remaining piece H to the bottom of the page, placing it ¼" from the bottom and ½" from the left edge.

5 Attach the specified photos (photos 2-3) to the appropriate areas, centering them on the mats.

JEANETTE'S TIP

Jazz up a layout by filling a design element with fun journaling in alternating fonts.

**Tone-on-Tone Stamping.** *For full Recipe and Technique see index pg. 120*

My Son

Elijah Coleman Bernardi

his smile
the way he laughs
chubby cheeks

boys will be boys

## Cutting Instructions

**B&T Paper**

| | |
|---|---|
| B 10 × 7 | F 5 × 10 |
| | SCRAP |

**Cardstock***

| | |
|---|---|
| E 12 × 4 | A 11 × 8 |
| | SCRAP |

**Cardstock***

| | |
|---|---|
| H 5 × 7 | D 7 × 5 |
| H 5 × 7 | |
| | SCRAP |

**Cardstock**

| |
|---|
| C 2 × 12 |
| G 2 × 12 |
| SCRAP |

*Identical papers

There are so many things I love about springtime. The flowers in bloom, the birds chirping, and warm breezes. I also love Easter. I love getting my girls all dressed up in their Easter dresses and taking pictures of them. Molly loves to pose so it works out perfect.

Easter 2005

*Cutting Instructions*

**B&T Paper**

K
5 × 12

C
6 × 9

A 1½ × 7    SCRAP    E 1½ × 3

**B&T Paper**

B 1½ × 12

F
1½ × 3

H ½ × 8½

M ½ × 8½

J ½ × 5

SCRAP

**Cardstock**

I
3 × 12

D
8 × 6

L 1 × 3    L 1 × 3    SCRAP

**Cardstock**

G
5 × 3

SCRAP

26

# Perfect Prelude

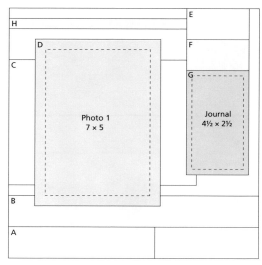

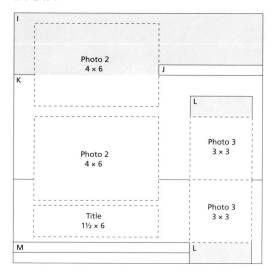

## Covering Chipboard Elements

**STEP 1** Attach chipboard element to back of cardstock. Cut closely around shape with scissors or a craft knife.

**STEP 2** Carefully sand or scissor distress (See tip on page 125) the edges to blend the paper to the chipboard.

*Layout Materials*

12" × 12" Base
Cardstock (2)

12" × 12"
Cardstock (2)

12" × 12" B&T
Paper (2)

*Left Page
Dimensions*

A  1½" × 7"
B  1½" × 12"
C  6" × 9"
D  8" × 6"
E  1½" × 3"
F  1½" × 3"
G  5" × 3"
H  ½" × 8½"

*Right Page
Dimensions*

I  3" × 12"
J  ½" × 5"
K  5" × 12"
L  1" × 3" (2)
M  ½" × 8½"

*Photo
Suggestions*

1  7" × 5"
2  4" × 6" (2)
3  3" × 3" (2)

*Suggested Title*

1  1½" × 6"

*Suggested
Journaling*

1  4½" × 2½"

**1** Using one 12" × 12" cardstock as your base, attach piece A to the bottom left corner of the page, keeping the edges flush.

**2** Attach piece B directly above piece A, keeping the side edges flush.

**3** Attach piece C to the left side of the page, placing it 2½" from the top, keeping the left edges flush.

**4** Attach piece D, placing it 1½" from the top and 1¼" from the left edge.

**5** Attach piece E to the top of the page, placing it ½" from the right edge, keeping the top edges flush.

**6** Attach piece F directly below piece E, keeping the edges flush.

**7** Attach piece G directly below piece F, keeping the edges flush.

**8** Attach piece H to the top left corner of the page, placing it ½" from the top, keeping the side edges flush with the page and piece E.

**9** Attach the specified photo (photo 1) to the appropriate area, centering it on the mat.

**1** Using one 12" × 12" cardstock as your base, attach piece I to the top of the page, keeping the edges flush.

**2** Attach piece J to the bottom right of piece I, keeping the edges flush.

**3** Attach piece K directly below pieces I and J, keeping the edges flush.

**4** Attach one piece L, placing it 4" from the top and ½" from the right edge.

**5** Attach remaining piece L to the bottom of the page, placing it ½" from the right edge, keeping the bottom edges flush.

**6** Attach piece M, placing it ½" from the bottom, keeping the side edges flush with the page and piece L.

**7** Attach the specified photos (photos 2-3) to the appropriate areas.

JEANETTE'S TIP

Stamp small words or patterns onto chipboard elements photo clips to add emphasis to your story.

*For full Recipe see index pg. 120*

# Powerful Trio

## Layout Materials

12" × 12" Base Cardstock (2)
12" × 12" Cardstock (2)
12" × 12" B&T Paper (3)

## Left Page Dimensions

A  1½" × 12"
B  8" × 2"
C  1" × 12"

## Right Page Dimensions

D  1½" × 12"
E  8" × 4" (2)
F  8" × 4"
G  3½" × 3½" (3)
H  1" × 12"

## Photo Suggestions

1  8" × 10"
2  3" × 3" (3)

## Suggested Title

1  1½" × 7½"

## Suggested Journaling

1  3½" × 11½"

## JEANETTE'S TIP

Hand-stitch tags and design elements to your page for pretty details—even a little bit goes a long way!

**Coloring Linen.** *For full Recipe and Technique see index pg. 121*

**LEFT**

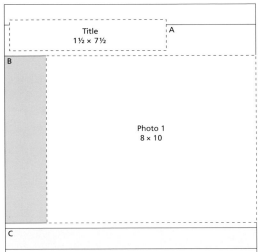

1  Using one 12" × 12" cardstock as your base, attach piece A, placing it 1" from the top of the page, keeping the side edges flush.

2  Attach piece B to the left side of the page, placing it 1½" from the bottom of the page, keeping the left edges flush.

3  Attach piece C, placing it ¼" from the bottom of the page, keeping the side edges flush.

4  Attach the specified photo (photo 1) to the appropriate area.

**RIGHT**

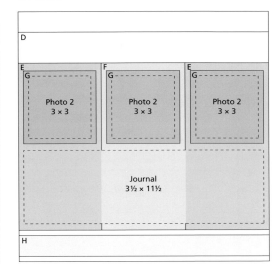

1  Using one 12" × 12" cardstock as your base, attach piece D, placing it 1" from the top of the page, keeping the side edges flush.

2  Attach one piece E directly below piece D, keeping the left edges flush. Attach remaining piece E directly below piece D, keeping the right edges flush.

3  Attach piece F between the two pieces E, keeping the edges flush.

4  Attach the three pieces G, placing them ¼" down from the top of pieces E, and F, with the left piece G ¼" from the left edge of the page, placing them ½" from each other.

5  Attach piece H, placing it ¼" from the bottom of the page, keeping the side edges flush.

6  Attach the specified photos (photos 2) to the appropriate areas, centering them on the mats.

**MOTHERS**

*Mother's day has always been my favorite day. I realize that it is probably every other mother's favorite day. But i agree with every other mother out there. Being a mother has been the accomplishment of my lifetime. I would never trade it for anything in the world.*

*God's most precious work of art, is the warmth and love of a mother's heart*

*I am so grateful every day that I look into the faces of my beautifull little girls. They make me smile in a world full of sadness. I believe that children are angels sent from above to teach parents and mothers like me how to love.*

## Cutting Instructions

**B&T Paper**

| A | 1½ × 12 |
|---|---------|
| D | 1½ × 12 |

SCRAP

**B&T Paper**

| C | 1 × 12 |
|---|--------|
| H | 1 × 12 |

SCRAP

**B&T Paper**

F
8 × 4

SCRAP

**Cardstock**

| B 8 × 2 | E 8 × 4 | E 8 × 4 |
|---------|---------|---------|

SCRAP

**Cardstock**

| G 3½ × 3½ | G 3½ × 3½ | G 3½ × 3½ |
|-----------|-----------|-----------|

SCRAP

What's the good of news if you haven't a sister to share it?
~Jenny DeVries

## Cutting Instructions

**B&T Paper**

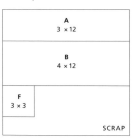

| | |
|---|---|
| **A** 3 × 12 | |
| **B** 4 × 12 | |
| **F** 3 × 3 | SCRAP |

**Cardstock**

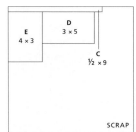

| | | |
|---|---|---|
| **E** 4 × 3 | **D** 3 × 5 | |
| | **C** ½ × 9 | SCRAP |

# Timeline

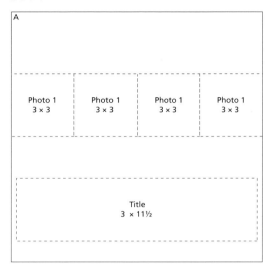

## Paper Quilting

### Layout Materials

12" × 12" Base
Cardstock (2)

12" × 12"
Cardstock (1)

12" × 12" B&T
Paper (1)

### Left Page Dimensions

A  3" × 12"

### Right Page Dimensions

B  4" × 12"
C  ½" × 9"
D  3" × 5"
E  4" × 3"
F  3" × 3"

### Photo Suggestions

1  3" × 3" (5)
2  2" × 2"

### Suggested Title

1  3" × 11½"

### Suggested Journaling

1  2½" × 4½"
2  2½" × 2"

**LEFT**

A

Photo 1
3 × 3 | Photo 1
3 × 3 | Photo 1
3 × 3 | Photo 1
3 × 3

Title
3 × 11½

1  Using one 12" × 12" cardstock as your base, attach piece A to the top of the page, keeping the edges flush.

2  Attach the specified photos (photos 1) to the appropriate areas.

**RIGHT**

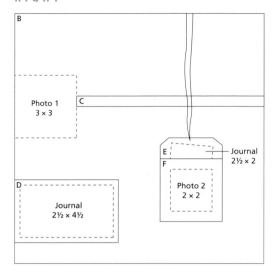

B

Photo 1
3 × 3

C

E    Journal
2½ × 2

F

Photo 2
2 × 2

D

Journal
2½ × 4½

1  Using one 12" × 12" cardstock as your base, attach piece B to the top of the page, keeping the edges flush.

2  Attach piece C directly below piece B, keeping the right edges flush.

3  Attach piece D to the left side of the page, placing it 1" from the bottom, keeping the left edges flush.

4  Cut the top corners of piece E diagonally to create a tag.

5  Attach piece F to the bottom of piece E, adhering only the side and bottom edges in order to form a pocket.

6  Attach a 12" piece of fiber or ribbon to pieces E and F tag as illustrated if desired.

7  Attach pieces E and F to the page, placing them 5½" from the top and 2" from the right edge of the page.

8  Attach the specified photos (photos 1-2) to the appropriate areas.

**STEP 1**  Cut two pieces of paper and thin batting to the desired size. Layer pieces of paper with batting between them.

**STEP 2**  Stitch paper in desired pattern. Embellish or distress as desired.

JEANETTE'S TIP

Photos can be added to the layout or to extra journaling spaces to further develop your story.

For full Recipe see index pg. 121

# Introduction

## Layout Materials

12" × 12" Base Cardstock (2)
12" × 12" Cardstock (2)
12" × 12" B&T Paper (2)

### Left Page Dimensions

A  11" × 6"
B  2½" × 3" (2" × 3" torn)
C  4" × 12"
D  12" × 4" (12" × 3½" torn)
E  2" × 12" (1½" × 12" torn)
F  2½" × 2½"
G  3½" × 4" (torn diagonal)

### Right Page Dimensions

H  4" × 12"
I  2" × 12" (1½" × 12" torn)
J  2½" × 2½" (2)
K  3" × 3"
L  ½" × 6"
M  6½" × 12" (6" × 12" torn)
N  3" × 2½" (3" × 2" torn)
O  6" × 4" (torn diagonal)

## Photo Suggestions

1  5" × 5" (3)
2  2" × 2" (3)

## Suggested Title

1  2" × 3"

## Suggested Journaling

1  4" × 3"

## JEANETTE'S TIP

For a unique look, stamp or print text onto twill as a journaling block or accent.

**Fraying Twill.** *For full Recipe and Technique see index pg. 121*

### LEFT

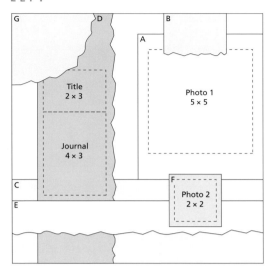

1  Decoratively tear or cut no more than ½" from pieces B, D, and E, as shown in the cutting diagrams. Decoratively tear or cut piece G in half diagonally as shown in the cutting diagrams.

2  Using one 12" × 12" cardstock as your base, attach piece A to the bottom right corner of the page, keeping the edges flush.

3  Attach piece B to the top of the page, placing it 1¾" from the right edge. Adhere only the top edge, in order to place a photo underneath.

4  Attach piece C to the bottom of the page, keeping the edges flush.

5  Attach piece D to the left side of the page, placing it 1¼" from the left edge, keeping the top and bottom edges flush.

6  Attach piece E to the bottom of the page, placing it 1" below the top of piece C and overlapping piece D, keeping the side edges flush.

7  Attach piece F to the lower right corner of the page, placing it 2" from the right and bottom edges.

8  Attach piece G to the top left corner of the page, keeping the edges flush.

9  Attach the specified photos (photos 1-2) to the appropriate areas, centering them on the mats.

### RIGHT

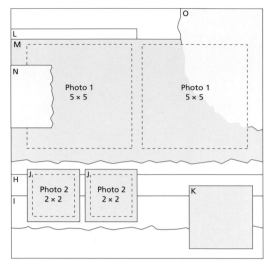

1  Decoratively tear or cut no more than ½" from pieces I, M, and N, as shown in the cutting diagrams. Decoratively tear or cut piece O in half diagonally as shown in the cutting diagram.

2  Using one 12" × 12" cardstock as your base, attach piece H to the bottom of the page, keeping the edges flush.

3  Attach piece I, placing it 1" below the top of piece H, keeping the side edges flush. (If completing the two-page layout be sure to line up the piece E and I strips across the pages.)

4  Attach both pieces J to the bottom left corner, placing them 2" from the bottom, ¾" from the left edge, and ¼" from each other.

5  Attach piece K to the bottom right corner of the page, placing it ½" from the bottom and right edges.

6  Attach piece L, placing it 1" from the top of the page, keeping the left edges flush.

7  Attach piece M directly below piece L, keeping the side edges flush.

8  Attach piece N, placing it 2¾" from the top edge of the page, keeping the left edges flush. Adhere only the left edge, in order to place a photo underneath.

9  Attach piece O to the top right corner of the page, Keeping the edges flush.

10  Attach the specified photos (photos 1-2) to the appropriate areas, centering them on the mats.

*Cutting Instructions*

**B&T Paper**

| |
|---|
| **H** 4 × 12 |
| **E** 2 × 12 |
| **A** 11 × 6 |
| **L** ½ × 6 |

**B&T Paper**

| |
|---|
| **C** 4 × 12 |
| **I** 2 × 12 |
| **O** 6 × 4 / **G** 3½ × 4 / **N** 3 × 2½ |
| **B** 2½ × 3 / SCRAP |

**Cardstock***

| |
|---|
| **M** 6½ × 12 |
| **F** 2½ × 2½ |
| **K** 3 × 3 / **J** 2½ × 2½ / SCRAP |

**Cardstock***

| |
|---|
| **D** 12 × 4 |
| SCRAP |

*Identical papers

33

my dog
MAX
from the build-a-bear workshop!!

1. Pick an animal
2. Fluff his body
3. Make a wish on his heart
Check-up

5. Wash and fluff his fur
6. Give him a name

A MIXTURE OF ELEMENTS COMES TOGETHER FOR A HARMONIOUS MEDLEY

····················· Cutting Instructions ·····················

B&T Paper

| | |
|---|---|
| | **B**<br>5 × 7 |
| **E**<br>12 × 3 | SCRAP |

Cardstock

| | |
|---|---|
| | **D**<br>7 × 7 |
| **A**<br>12 × 5 | SCRAP |

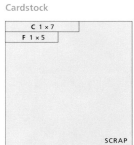

Cardstock

| | |
|---|---|
| **C** 1 × 7 | |
| **F** 1 × 5 | |
| | SCRAP |

# Medley

*Layout Materials*

12" × 12" Base Cardstock (2)

12" × 12" Cardstock (2)

12" × 12" B&T Paper (1)

*Left Page Dimensions*

A 12" × 5"
B 5" × 7"
C 1" × 7"

*Right Page Dimensions*

D 7" × 7"
E 12" × 3"
F 1" × 5"

*Photo Suggestions*

1 6" × 4" (2)
2 3" × 3" (4)
3 6" × 3" (2)
4 4" × 6"

*Suggested Title*

1 4" × 6"

*Suggested Journaling*

1 1" × 4" (6)

LEFT

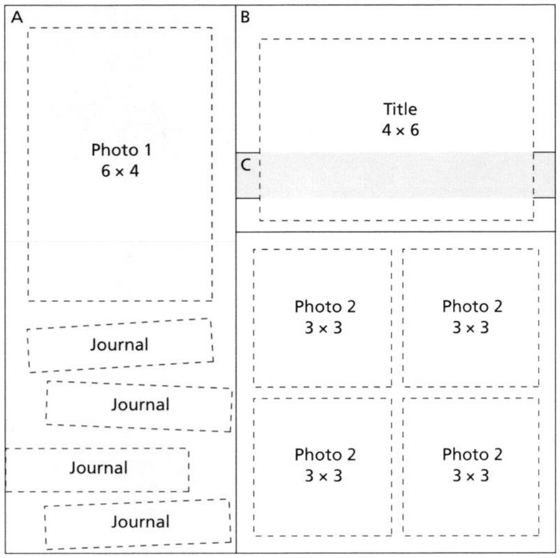

A
B
Title
4 × 6
C
Photo 1
6 × 4
Journal
Journal
Journal
Journal
Photo 2
3 × 3
Photo 2
3 × 3
Photo 2
3 × 3
Photo 2
3 × 3


1 Using one 12" × 12" cardstock as your base, attach piece A to the left side of the page, keeping the edges flush.

2 Attach piece B to the top right corner of the page, keeping the edges flush.

3 Attach piece C, placing it ½" from the bottom of piece B, keeping the side edges flush.

4 Attach the specified photos (photos 1-2) to the appropriate areas.

RIGHT

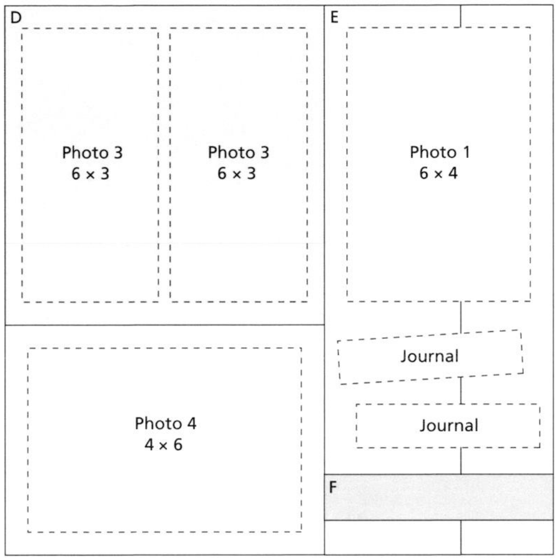

D
E
Photo 3
6 × 3
Photo 3
6 × 3
Photo 1
6 × 4
Journal
Journal
Photo 4
4 × 6
F


1 Using one 12" × 12" cardstock as your base, attach piece D to the top left corner of the page, keeping the edges flush.

2 Attach piece E directly to the right of piece D, keeping the edges flush.

3 Attach piece F to the right side of the page, placing it ¾" from the bottom, keeping the right edges flush.

4 Attach the specified photos (photos 1, 3, and 4) to the appropriate areas.

**Stitching with Waxy Flax**

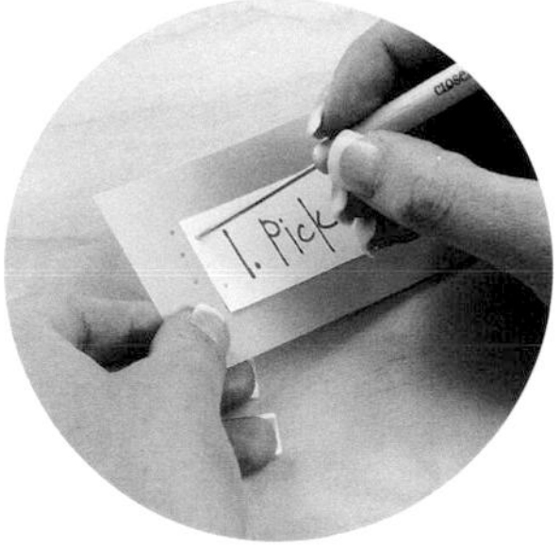

1. Pick


STEP 1 Adhere journaling strip to your layout. Determine the type of stitch design you would like to us. (Experiment on scrap paper.) Punch holes with piercing tool.

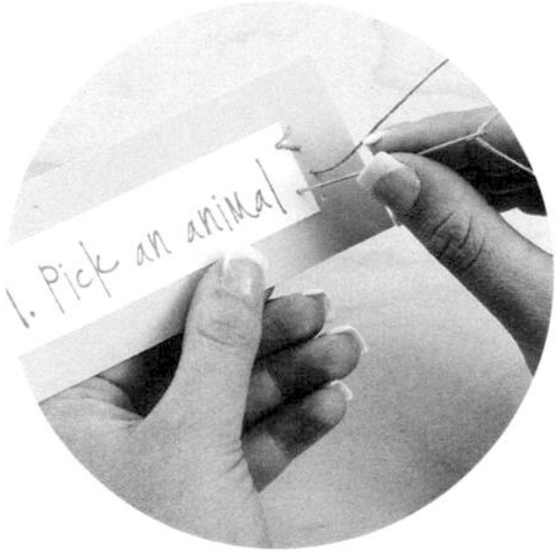

1. Pick an animal


STEP 2 Stitch desired design into pre-punched holes. Tie thread off on the back of the layout and tape using an acid-free tape to secure stitching.

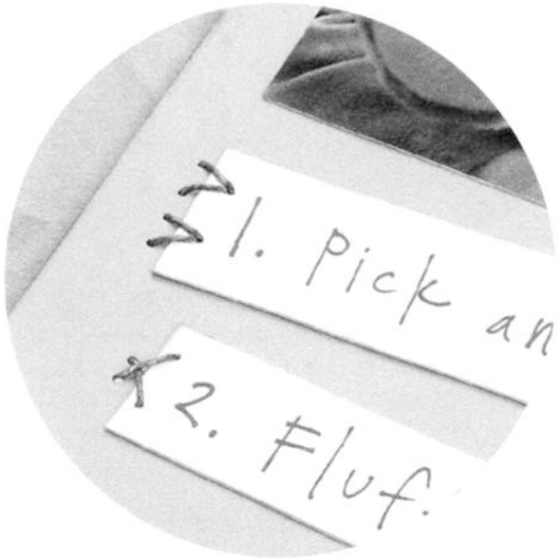

1. Pick an
2. Fluf


JEANETTE'S TIP

Numbering your pictures and journaling blocks is a fun way to explain events, especially with a series of photos.

*For full Recipe see index pg. 121*

# Serenade

## Layout Materials

12" × 12" Base Cardstock (2)
12" × 12" Cardstock (3)
12" × 12" B&T Paper (3)

## Left Page Dimensions

A  12" × 3½"
B  2" × 12"
C  4" × 8" (3½" × 8" torn)
D  4" × 8½" (3½" × 8½" torn)
E  2" × 8½" (1½" × 8½" torn)
F  4" × 4" (torn diagonally)
G  6" × 2½" (2)

## Right Page Dimensions

H  8" × 12"
I  6½" × 5"
J  6½" × 8" (6½" × 7½" torn)
K  6" × 2½"
L  2" × 12" (1½" × 12" torn)
M  2" × 4" (2) (1½" × 4" torn)
N  4" × 4" (torn diagonally)

## Photo Suggestions

1  2½" × 2½" (3)
2  5" × 7"
3  6" × 4" (2)

## Suggested Title

1  1¾" × 4"

## Suggested Journaling

1  4½" × 2"

**JEANETTE'S TIP**

Quotes make a fun addition to any page.

**File Folders.** *For full Recipe and Technique see index pg. 121*

**LEFT**

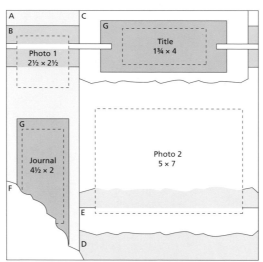

**1** Decoratively tear or cut no more than ½" from pieces C, D, and E as shown in the cutting diagrams. Decoratively tear or cut piece F (N) in half diagonally as shown in the cutting diagrams.

**2** Using one 12" × 12" cardstock as your base, attach piece A to the left side of the page, keeping the edges flush.

**3** Attach piece B across the top of the page, placing it ¾" from the top edge, keeping the side edges flush.

**4** Attach piece C to the top of the page, keeping the left edge flush against piece A and the top edges flush.

**5** Attach piece D to the bottom right corner of the page, keeping the edges flush.

**6** Attach piece E across the center of piece D, keeping the side edges flush.

**7** Attach piece F to the lower left corner, adhering only the left and bottom edges in order to form a pocket.

**8** Attach one piece G to the top of the page, centered over piece C, fastening with ribbon if desired. Insert remaining piece G into the piece F pocket in the bottom left corner.

**9** Attach the specified photos (photos 1-2) to the appropriate areas.

**RIGHT**

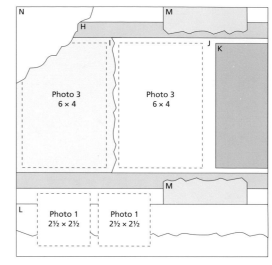

**1** Decoratively tear or cut no more than ½" from pieces J, L, and M (2) as shown in the cutting diagrams. Decoratively tear or cut piece N (F) in half diagonally as shown in the cutting diagrams.

**2** Using one 12" × 12" cardstock as your base, attach piece H to the page, ¾" from the top edge, keeping the side edges flush.

**3** Attach piece I to the left side of piece H, placing it ¾" down from the top of piece H, keeping the left edges flush.

**4** Attach piece J to the right side of piece H, placing it ¾" down from the top of piece H, and slightly overlapping piece I, keeping the right edges flush.

**5** Attach piece K to the right side of piece J, centering it from top to bottom, keeping the right edges flush.

**6** Attach piece L across the bottom of the page, placing it approximately 1" from the bottom edge, keeping the side edges flush. (If completing the two-page layout be sure to line up the piece E and L strips across the pages.)

**7** Attach one piece M to the top of the page, placing it 1" from the right edge, keeping the top edges flush. Attach remaining piece M directly above piece L, placing it 1" from the right edge.

**8** Attach piece N to the top left corner, adhering only the top and side edges in order to form a photo corner.

**9** Attach the specified photos (photos 1 and 3) to the appropriate areas.

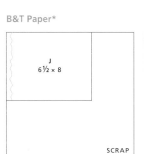
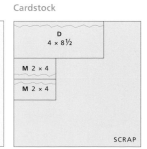

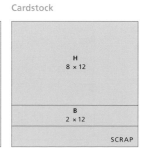

**ONE MAIN FOCAL POINT SERENADES SMALLER ELEMENTS IN BEAUTIFUL STYLE**

## Cutting Instructions

**B&T Paper\***

- L 2 × 12
- C 4 × 8
- F 4 × 4
- N
- E 2 × 8½
- SCRAP

**B&T Paper\***

- J 6½ × 8
- SCRAP

**B&T Paper**

- I 6½ × 5
- A 12 × 3½
- SCRAP

**Cardstock**

- D 4 × 8½
- M 2 × 4
- M 2 × 4
- SCRAP

**Cardstock**

- H 8 × 12
- B 2 × 12
- SCRAP

**Cardstock**

- G 6 × 2½
- G 6 × 2½
- K 6 × 2½
- SCRAP

*\*Identical papers*

37

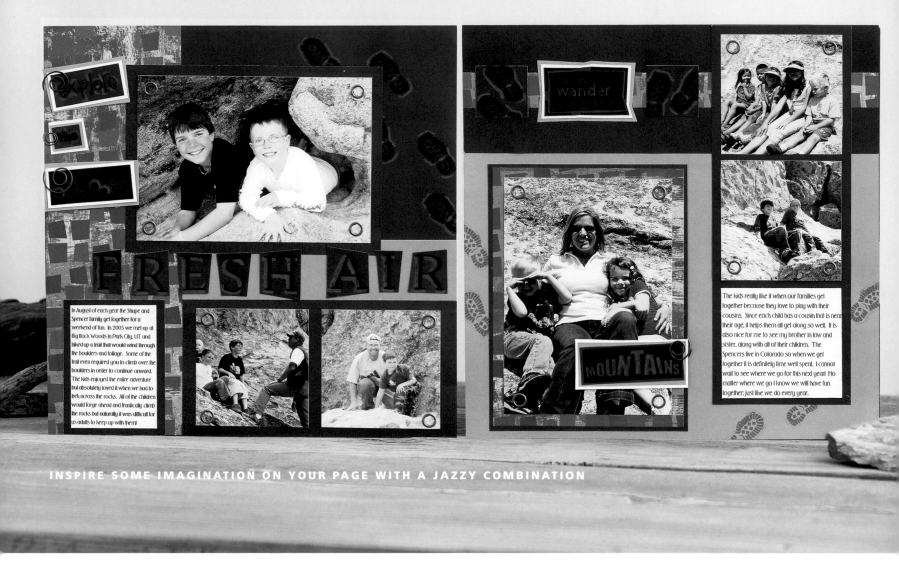

explore the outdoors

FRESH AIR

In August of each year the Shupe and Spencer family get together for a weekend of fun. In 2005 we met up at Big Rock Woods in Park City, UT and hiked up a trail that would wind through the boulders and foliage. Some of the trail even required you to climb over the boulders in order to continue onward. The kids enjoyed the entire adventure but absolutely loved it when we had to trek across the rocks. All of the children would forge ahead and frantically climb the rocks but naturally it was difficult for us adults to keep up with them!

wander

MOUNTAINS

The kids really like it when our families get together because they love to play with their cousins. Since each child has a cousin that is near their age, it helps them all get along so well. It is also nice for me to see my brother in law and sister, along with all of their children. The Spencers live in Colorado so when we get together it is definitely time well spent. I cannot wait to see where we go for this next year! No matter where we go I know we will have fun together; just like we do every year.

**INSPIRE SOME IMAGINATION ON YOUR PAGE WITH A JAZZY COMBINATION**

················· *Cutting Instructions* ·······································································

B&T Paper

A 12 × 4

J 7½ × 5½

G 1 × 12

SCRAP

Cardstock

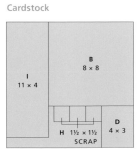

F 3¾ × 12

E 4 × 8

C 5½ × 7½

SCRAP

Cardstock

I 11 × 4

B 8 × 8

H 1½ × 1½

D 4 × 3

SCRAP

# Jazzy Combination

**Waterbrushing**

## Layout Materials

12" × 12" Base
Cardstock (2)

12" × 12"
Cardstock (2)

12" × 12" B&T
Paper (1)

## Left Page Dimensions

A  12" × 4"
B  8" × 8"
C  5½" × 7½"
D  4" × 3"
E  4" × 8"

## Right Page Dimensions

F  3¾" × 12"
G  1" × 12"
H  1½" × 1½" (3)
I  11" × 4"
J  7½" × 5½"

## Photo Suggestions

1  5" × 7"
2  3½" × 3½" (4)
3  7" × 5"

## Suggested Title

1  1" × 7½"

## Suggested Journaling

1  3½" × 2½"
2  3¼" × 3½"

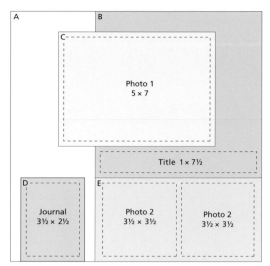

Photo 1
5 × 7

Title 1 x 7½

Journal
3½ x 2½

Photo 2
3½ × 3½

Photo 2
3½ × 3½

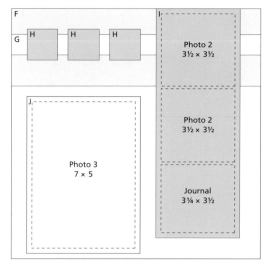

Photo 2
3½ × 3½

Photo 2
3½ × 3½

Photo 3
7 × 5

Journal
3¼ × 3½

1  Using one 12" × 12" cardstock as your base, attach piece A to the left side of the page, keeping the edges flush.

2  Attach piece B to the top right corner of the page, keeping the edges flush.

3  Attach piece C, placing it 1" from the top and 2¼" from the left edge of the page.

4  Attach piece D to the bottom left corner of the page, placing it ½" from the left edge, keeping the bottom edges flush.

5  Attach piece E to the bottom right corner of the page, keeping the edges flush.

6  Attach the specified photos (photos 1-2) to the appropriate areas, centering them on the mats.

1  Using one 12" × 12" cardstock as your base, attach piece F to the top of the page, keeping the edges flush.

2  Attach piece G to the center of piece F, placing it 1¼" from the top, keeping the side edges flush.

3  Attach the three pieces H across the left side of piece G, placing them ¾" from the left edge and ½" from each other.

4  Attach piece I to the top right side of the page, placing it 1" from the right edge, keeping the top edges flush.

5  Attach piece J, placing it ¾" from the left edge and ¼" from the bottom edge of the page.

6  Attach the specified photos (photos 2-3) to the appropriate areas, centering them on the mats.

**STEP 1** Stamp image in desired color. Using a coordinating watercolor pencil, draw around stamp to create a shadow.

**STEP 2** Using a waterbrush, brush the drawn shadow away from the stamped image with even strokes.

### JEANETTE'S TIP

Anchor your photos to your layout using embellishments as photo corners.

*For full Recipe see index pg. 121*

# Ensemble Piece

## Layout Materials

12" × 12" Base Cardstock (2)
12" × 12" Cardstock (3)
12" × 12" B&T Paper (3)

## Photo Suggestions

1  4" × 6"
2  4" × 4" (4)
3  6" × 4"

## Left Page Dimensions

A  6" × 6"
B  5" × 6"
C  8" × 7½"
D  4½" × 6½"
E  2" × 8"
F  2" × 2"

## Suggested Title

1  1½" × 5"

## Suggested Journaling

1  1½" × 3"

## Right Page Dimensions

G  5" × 6"
H  6" × 6"
I  12" × 4"
J  8" × 7½"
K  6½" × 4½"
L  6½" × 2"
M  2" × 3½"

**LEFT**

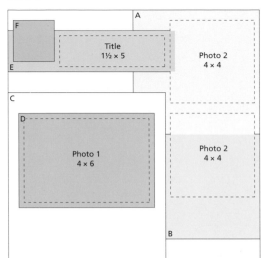

**RIGHT**

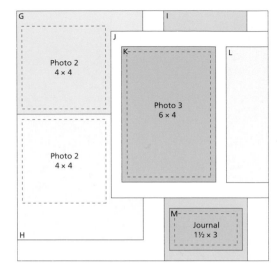

**1**  Using one 12" × 12" cardstock as your base, attach piece A to the top right corner of the page, keeping the edges flush.

**2**  Attach piece B directly below piece A, keeping the edges flush.

**3**  Attach piece C to the bottom left corner of the page, keeping the edges flush.

**4**  Attach piece D to piece C, placing it 1" from the top of piece C and ½" from the left edge of the page.

**5**  Attach piece E to the left side of the page, placing it 1" from the top, keeping the left edges flush.

**6**  Attach piece F over piece E, placing it ½" from the top and ¼" from the left edge of the page.

**7**  Attach the specified photos (photos 1-2) to the appropriate areas, centering them on the mats.

**1**  Using one 12" × 12" cardstock as your base, attach piece G to the top left corner of the page, keeping the edges flush.

**2**  Attach piece H directly below piece G, keeping the left edges flush.

**3**  Attach piece I down the right side of the page, placing it 1" from the right edge, keeping the top and bottom edges flush.

**4**  Attach piece J to the right side of the page, placing it 1" from the top, keeping the right edges flush.

**5**  Attach piece K to piece J, placing it ¾" from the top of piece J and ½" from the left edge of piece J.

**6**  Attach piece L to the right side of the page, placing it ¾" from the top of piece J, keeping the right edges flush.

**7**  Attach piece M to the bottom of piece I, placing it ½" from the bottom edge and centered on piece I from side to side.

**8**  Attach the specified photos (photos 2-3) to the appropriate areas, centering them on the mats.

PUT TOGETHER AN ENSEMBLE PIECE WITH A COMBINATION OF FOCAL POINTS

Cutting Instructions

B&T Paper*

C
8 × 7½

SCRAP

B&T Paper*

J
8 × 7½

SCRAP

B&T Paper

A
6 × 6

L
6½ × 2

H
6 × 6

SCRAP

Cardstock

B
5 × 6

G
5 × 6

SCRAP

Cardstock

E
2 × 8

I
12 × 4

SCRAP

Cardstock

K
6½ × 4½

D
4½ × 6½

M
2 × 3½

F
2 × 2

SCRAP

*Identical papers

41

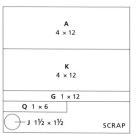
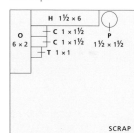
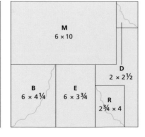
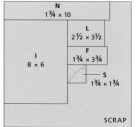

freedom

Scott's class trip to Philadelphia, Pennsylvania. The kids were studying American history and this was a first class learning experience for them. Scott couldn't stop talking about how cool the Liberty Bell was with "that huge crack"!!

MAY 2005

**A LARGE PHOTO IS SUPPORTED WITH ACCOMPANYING SMALL PHOTOS AND ACCENTS**

········· *Cutting Instructions* ·········

**B&T Paper**

| | |
|---|---|
| **A** 4 × 12 | |
| **K** 4 × 12 | |
| **G** 1 × 12 | |
| **Q** 1 × 6 | |
| **J** 1½ × 1½ | SCRAP |

**B&T Paper**

**H** 1½ × 6
**O** 6 × 2
**C** 1 × 1½
**C** 1 × 1½
**P** 1½ × 1½
**T** 1 × 1
SCRAP

**Cardstock**

**M** 6 × 10
**D** 2 × 2½
**B** 6 × 4¼
**E** 6 × 3¾
**R** 2¾ × 4
SCRAP

**Cardstock**

**N** 1¾ × 10
**L** 2½ × 3½
**I** 8 × 6
**F** 1¾ × 3¾
**S** 1¾ × 1¾
SCRAP

42

# Concerto

## Resist Embossing

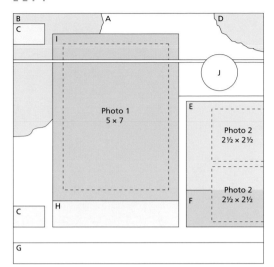

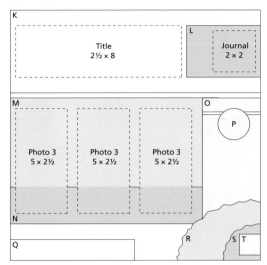

**STEP 1** Stamp an image with embossing ink. Cover image with clear embossing powder, tapping off excess. Heat with a heat tool until powder melts.

### Layout Materials

12" × 12" Base Cardstock (2)

12" × 12" Cardstock (2)

12" × 12" B&T Paper (2)

### Left Page Dimensions

A  4" × 12"
B  6" × 4¼" (torn diagonally)
C  1" × 1½" (2)
D  2" × 2½" (torn diagonally)
E  6" × 3¾"
F  1¾" × 3¾"
G  1" × 12"
H  1½" × 6"
I  8" × 6"
J  1½" × 1½" circle

### Right Page Dimensions

K  4" × 12"
L  2½" × 3½"
M  6" × 10"
N  1¾" × 10"
O  6" × 2"
P  1½" × 1½" circle
Q  1" × 6"
R  2¾" × 4" (torn diagonally)
S  1¾" × 1¾" (torn diagonally)
T  1" × 1"

### Photo Suggestions

1  5" × 7"
2  2½" × 2½" (2)
3  5" × 2½" (3)

### Suggested Title

1  2½" × 8"

### Suggested Journaling

1  2" × 2"

**1** Decoratively tear or cut pieces B and D in half diagonally as shown in the cutting diagrams.

**2** Using one 12" × 12" cardstock as your base, attach piece A to the top of the page, keeping the edges flush.

**3** Attach piece B to the top left corner of the page, keeping the edges flush.

**4** Attach one piece C, placing it 1¾" from the bottom, keeping the left edges flush. Attach remaining piece C, placing it ½" from the top, keeping the left edges flush.

**5** Attach piece D to the top right corner of the page, keeping the edges flush.

**6** Attach piece E to the right side of the page, placing it 1¾" from the bottom, keeping the right edges flush.

**7** Attach piece F to the bottom of piece E, keeping the right edges flush.

**8** Attach piece G to the bottom edge of the page, keeping the edges flush.

**9** Attach piece H placing it 1¾" from the left and bottom edges of the page.

**10** Attach piece I directly above piece H.

**11** Attach piece J with ribbon to the top right of the page.

**12** Attach the specified photos (photos 1-2) to the appropriate areas, centering them on the mats.

**1** Decoratively tear or cut pieces R and S in half diagonally as shown in the cutting diagrams.

**2** Using one 12" × 12" cardstock as your base, attach piece K to the top of the page, keeping the edges flush.

**3** Attach piece L to the right side of piece K, placing it ¾" from the top, keeping the right edges flush.

**4** Attach piece M to the left side of the page, placing it 1¾" from the bottom, keeping the left edges flush.

**5** Attach piece N to the bottom of piece M, keeping the left edges flush.

**6** Attach piece P to the top of piece O with ribbon.

**7** Attach pieces O and P to the right side of the page, keeping the right edges flush.

**8** Attach piece Q to the bottom left corner of the page, keeping the edges flush.

**9** Attach piece R to the bottom right corner of the page, keeping the outside edges flush.

**10** Attach piece S to the right corner of piece R, keeping the edges flush.

**11** Attach piece T to piece S, placing it ¼" from the bottom edge, keeping the right edges flush.

**12** Attach the specified photos (photos 3) to the appropriate areas.

**STEP 2** Sponge ink onto image, wiping it off as you go. Ink will stay in the recesses, creating a relief image.

### JEANETTE'S TIP

Distress the edges of your photo mats to give your layout a rustic feel.

*For full Recipe see index pg. 122*

# Three-Part Harmony

## Layout Materials

12" × 12" Base Cardstock (2)
12" × 12" Cardstock (3)
12" × 12" B&T Paper (2)

### Left Page Dimensions

A  2½" × 2½"
B  1½" × 9½"
C  1½" × 12"
D  ½" × 12"
E  4" × 6"
   (3½" × 6" torn)
F  7" × 5"

### Right Page Dimensions

G  2" × 2"
H  1½" × 12"
I  6" × 12"
J  1½" × 12"
K  3" × 3"
L  12" × 2½"
   (12" × 2" torn)
M  7" × 5" (2)

## Photo Suggestions

1  6" × 4" (3)
2  3" × 2½" (2)
3  2" × 2"

## Suggested Title

1  2½" × 5½"

## Suggested Journaling

1  1" × 9"

### JEANETTE'S TIP

Date stamps serve double duty—they're
informative and decorative at the same time.

**Make Your Own Buckle.** *For full Recipe and
Technique see index pg. 122*

### LEFT

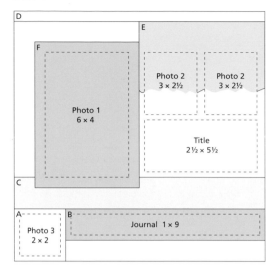

1  Decoratively tear or cut no more than ½" from
piece E as shown in the cutting diagrams.

2  Using one 12" × 12" cardstock as your base, attach
piece A to the bottom left corner of the page, keeping
the edges flush.

3  Attach piece B directly to the right of piece A,
placing it 1" from the bottom of the page, keeping
the right edges flush.

4  Attach piece C directly above pieces A and B,
keeping the side edges flush.

5  Attach piece D to the top of the page, keeping the
edges flush.

6  Attach piece E to the right side of the page directly
below piece D, keeping the right edges flush.

7  Attach piece F directly to the left of piece E, placing
it 1½" from the top of the page.

8  Attach the specified photos (photos 1-3) to the
appropriate areas, centering them on the mats.

### RIGHT

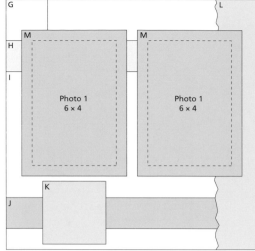

1  Decoratively tear or cut no more than ½" from
piece L as shown in the cutting diagrams.

2  Using one 12" × 12" cardstock as your base,
attach piece G to the top left corner of the page,
keeping the edges flush.

3  Attach piece H across the page directly below
piece G, keeping the side edges flush.

4  Attach piece I directly below piece H, keeping the
side edges flush.

5  Attach piece J directly below piece I, keeping the
side edges flush.

6  Attach piece K, placing it 1½" from the left edge
and ¼" from the bottom of the page.

7  Attach piece L to the right side of the page,
keeping the edges flush.

8  Attach one piece M, placing it 1½" from the top
and ¾" from the left edge of the page. Attach
remaining piece M, placing it 1½" from
the top and ¾" from the right edge of the page.

9  Attach the specified photos (photos 1) to the
appropriate areas, centering them on the mats.

STAN & AMY

San Francisco

To celebrate our tenth anniversary Stan and I decided to take a trip to San Francisco. We spent five days exploring the city and taking in all the sites. We went to the wharf and checked out the local fish markets. We rented bikes and took a tour of San Francisco, stopping at the Golden Gate Bridge. Of course we had to go to the Ghirardelli Chocolate Factory. Stan loves chocolate so we stocked up on delicious chocolate and got a few things for the kids as well. We also went on a tour of Alcatraz, which was very interesting. It's hard to imagine we've been married for ten years already. We had so much fun.

APRIL 2006

## Cutting Instructions

**B&T Paper**

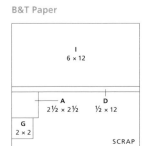

I
6 × 12

A
2½ × 2½

D
½ × 12

G
2 × 2

SCRAP

**B&T Paper**

C 1½ ×12

H 1½ ×12

SCRAP

**Cardstock**

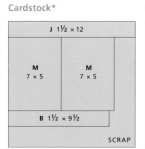

E
4 × 6

K
3 × 3

L
12 × 2½

SCRAP

**Cardstock***

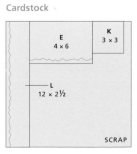

J 1½ × 12

M
7 × 5

M
7 × 5

B 1½ × 9½

SCRAP

**Cardstock***

F
7 × 5

SCRAP

*Identical papers*

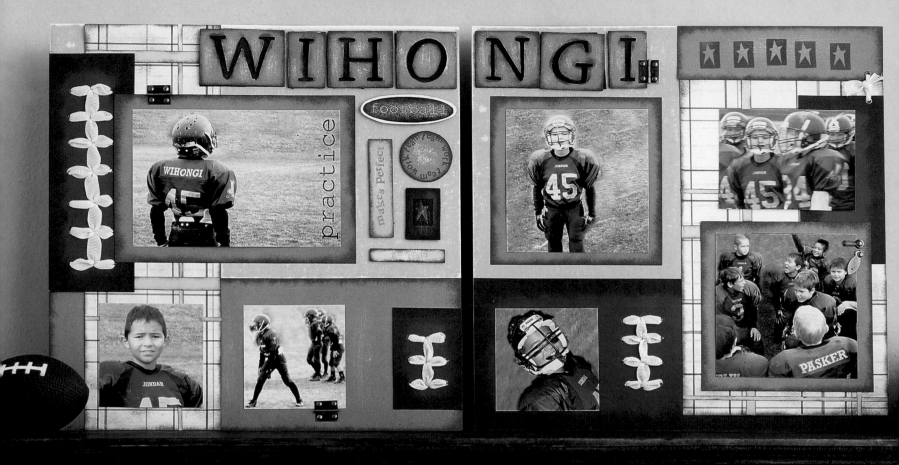

GRACEFUL, STATELY, AND FULL OF ELEGANCE TO SHOW OFF YOUR MEMORIES

---

*Cutting Instructions*

**B&T Paper**

- B 12 × 4
- H 10 × 6
- SCRAP

**Cardstock**

- F 4½ × 12
- E 3 × 2
- I 5 × 2½
- C 7 × 2½
- SCRAP

**Cardstock***

- A 4½ × 12
- D 5 × 7
- J 5 × 5
- G 1½ × 6
- SCRAP

**Cardstock***

- J 5 × 5
- SCRAP

*Identical papers

46

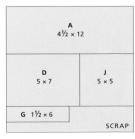
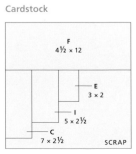

# Minuet

## Layout Materials

12" × 12" Base
Cardstock (2)

12" × 12"
Cardstock (3)

12" × 12" B&T
Paper (1)

### Left Page Dimensions

A  4½" × 12"
B  12" × 4"
C  7" × 2½"
D  5" × 7"
E  3" × 2"

### Right Page Dimensions

F  4½" × 12"
G  1½" × 6"
H  10" × 6"
I  5" × 2½"
J  5" × 5" (2)

### Photo Suggestions

1  4" × 6"
2  3" × 3" (3)
3  4" × 4" (2)
4  3" × 4"

### Suggested Title

1  1½" × 12"

### Suggested Journaling

1  5" × 3"

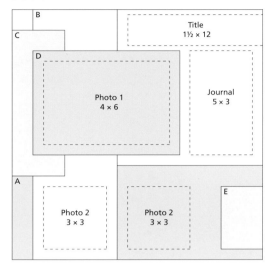

Title
1½ × 12

B
C
D

Photo 1
4 × 6

Journal
5 × 3

A

Photo 2
3 × 3

Photo 2
3 × 3

E

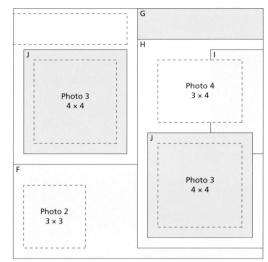

RIGHT

G
H
J

Photo 3
4 × 4

Photo 4
3 × 4

I

J

Photo 3
4 × 4

F

Photo 2
3 × 3

**1**  Using one 12" × 12" cardstock as your base, attach piece A to the bottom of the page, keeping the edges flush.

**2**  Attach piece B, placing it 1" from the left edge of the page, keeping the top and bottom edges flush.

**3**  Attach piece C to the left side of the page, placing it 1" from the top, keeping the left edges flush.

**4**  Attach piece D to pieces B and C, placing it 2" from the top and 1" from the left edge.

**5**  Attach piece E to the bottom right corner of the page, placing it ½" from the bottom, keeping the right edges flush.

**6**  Attach the specified photos (photos 1-2) to the appropriate areas, centering them on the mats.

**1**  Using one 12" × 12" cardstock as your base, attach piece F to the bottom of the page, keeping the edges flush.

**2**  Attach piece G to the top right corner of the page, keeping the edges flush.

**3**  Attach piece H directly below piece G, keeping the right edges flush.

**4**  Attach piece I to the right side of piece H, placing it 2" from the top of the page, keeping the right edges flush.

**5**  Attach one piece J, placing it 2" from the top and ½" from the left edge of the page. Attach remaining piece J, placing it ½" from the right edge and 1" from the bottom of the page.

**6**  Attach the specified photos (photos 2-4) to the appropriate areas, centering them on the mats.

## Bending Stamps

**STEP 1**  Choose a long, narrow stamp image such as a word or phrase.

**STEP 2**  Curve the stamp as you attach it to the block. Ink and stamp as normal.

### JEANETTE'S TIP

Sometimes the decorative detail choices help tell your story, such as the handsewn ribbon patterns that tie in the football theme of the layout.

*For full Recipe see index pg. 122*

# Dynamic Duo

## Layout Materials

12" × 12" Base Cardstock (2)
12" × 12" Cardstock (2)
12" × 12" B&T Paper (2)

## Left Page Dimensions

A  4" × 6"
B  12" × 2"
C  12" × 4"
D  3" × 3" (2)
E  4" × 3"
F  7" × 5"

## Right Page Dimensions

G  8" × 2"
H  8" × 4"
I   3" × 3" (2)
J  4" × 12"
K  2" × 9½"
L  7" × 5"

## Photo Suggestions

1  6" × 4" (2)
2  2½" × 2½" (4)
3  3½" × 2½"

## Suggested Title

1  11" × 1"

## Suggested Journaling

1  1" × 8½"

## JEANETTE'S TIP

Adjust photo mat from a ¼" border to an ⅛" border by adding ¼" to both the length and width of the photo.

**Creating Fun Photo Mats.** *For full Recipe and Technique see index pg. 122*

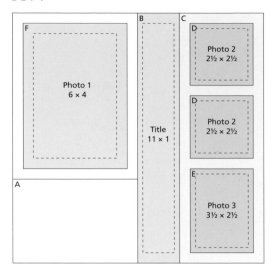

**LEFT**

1  Using one 12" × 12" cardstock as your base, attach piece A to the bottom left corner of the page, keeping the edges flush.

2  Attach piece B directly to the right of piece A, keeping the edges flush.

3  Attach piece C to the right side of the page, keeping the edges flush.

4  Attach the two pieces D to piece C, centered from side to side, ½" from the top and each other.

5  Attach piece E to piece C, centered ½" below the second piece D.

6  Attach piece F to the page, placing it ½" from the top and left edges.

7  Attach the specified photos (photos 1-3) to the appropriate areas, centering them on the mats.

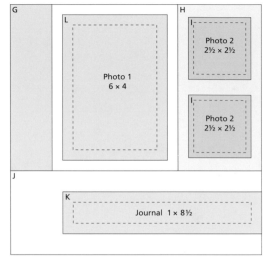

**RIGHT**

1  Using one 12" × 12" cardstock as your base, attach piece G to the top left corner of the page, keeping the edges flush.

2  Attach piece H to the top right corner of the page, keeping the edges flush.

3  Attach the two pieces I to piece H, centered from top to bottom and side to side.

4  Attach piece J to the bottom of the page, keeping the edges flush.

5  Attach piece K to piece J, placing it 1" from the top of piece J, keeping the right edges flush.

6  Attach piece L, placing it ½" from the top of the page and ½" from the right edge of piece G.

7  Attach the specified photos (photos 1-2) to the appropriate areas, centering them on the mats.

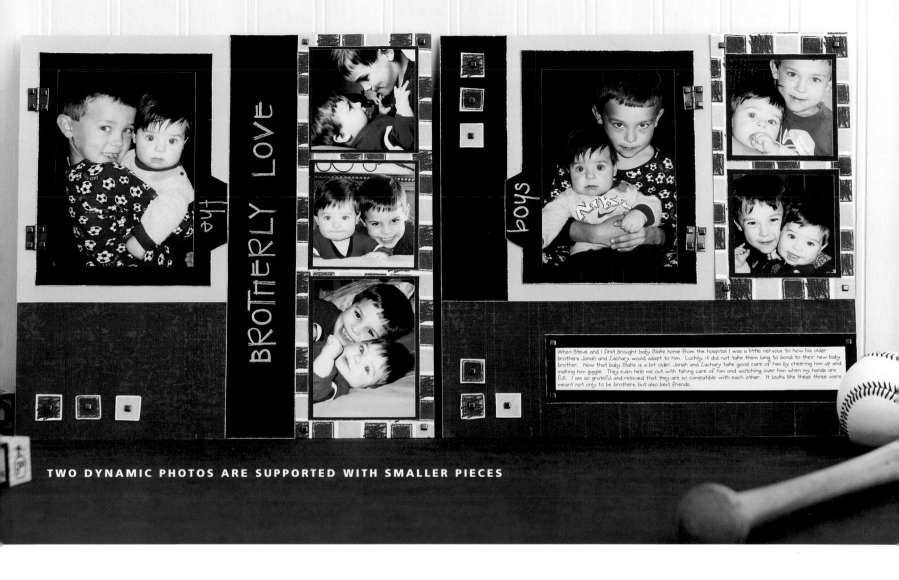

BROTHERLY LOVE

the

boys

When Steve and I first brought baby Blake home from the hospital I was a little nervous to how his older brothers Jonah and Zachary would adapt to him. Luckily, it did not take them long to bond to their new baby brother. Now that baby Blake is a bit older, Jonah and Zachary take good care of him by cheering him up and making him giggle. They even help me out with taking care of him and watching over him when my hands are full. I am so grateful and relieved that they are so compatible with each other. It looks like these three were meant not only to be brothers, but also best friends.

**TWO DYNAMIC PHOTOS ARE SUPPORTED WITH SMALLER PIECES**

........... *Cutting Instructions* ...........................

**B&T Paper**

| | |
|---|---|
| **J** 4 × 12 | |
| **A** 4 × 6 | |
| | SCRAP |

**B&T Paper**

| | |
|---|---|
| **C** 12 × 4 | **H** 8 × 4 |
| | SCRAP |

**Cardstock**

| | | |
|---|---|---|
| **B** 12 × 2 | **F** 7 × 5 | **L** 7 × 5 |
| | **K** 2 × 9½ | |
| | **G** 8 × 2 | |
| | | SCRAP |

**Cardstock**

| | |
|---|---|
| **D** 3 × 3 | **D** 3 × 3 |
| **I** 3 × 3 | **I** 3 × 3 |
| **E** 4 × 3 | |
| | SCRAP |

"WHEN MY HANDS ARE BUSY,
MY HEART IS FULL."

Create

## Cutting Instructions

**B&T Paper**

| | |
|---|---|
| **A** 2 × 12 | |
| **C** 1 × 12 | |
| **F** 12 × 2 | |
| **E** 2 × 7 | |
| | SCRAP |

**B&T Paper**

| |
|---|
| **B** 3 × 12 |
| **G** 12 × 3 |
| SCRAP |

**Cardstock**

| | |
|---|---|
| **D** 7 × 5 | **H** 5 × 7 |
| | |
| | SCRAP |

# Monologue

© 2007 JRL PUBLICATIONS

## LEFT

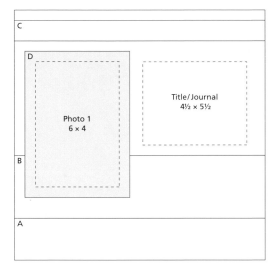

## RIGHT

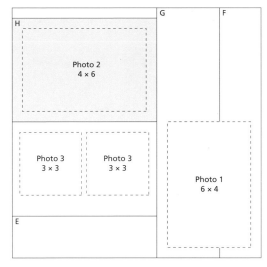

*Layout Materials*

12" × 12" Base
Cardstock (2)

12" × 12"
Cardstock (1)

12" × 12" B&T
Paper (2)

*Left Page
Dimensions*

A 2" × 12"
B 3" × 12"
C 1" × 12"
D 7" × 5"

*Right Page
Dimensions*

E 2" × 7"
F 12" × 2"
G 12" × 3"
H 5" × 7"

*Photo
Suggestions*

1 6" × 4" (2)
2 4" × 6"
3 3" × 3" (2)

*Suggested Title/
Journaling*

1 4½" × 5½"

**LEFT**

1  Using one 12" × 12" cardstock as your base, attach piece A to the bottom of the page, keeping the edges flush.

2  Attach piece B directly above piece A, keeping the edges flush.

3  Attach piece C to the top of the page, placing it ½" from the top, keeping the side edges flush.

4  Attach piece D to the page, placing it 2" from the top and ½" from the left edge.

5  Attach the specified photo (photo 1) to the appropriate area, centering it on the mat.

**RIGHT**

1  Using one 12" × 12" cardstock as your base, attach piece E to the bottom left corner of the page, keeping the edges flush.

2  Attach piece F to the right side of the page, keeping the edges flush.

3  Attach piece G directly to the left of piece F, keeping the edges flush.

4  Attach piece H to the left side of the page, placing it ½" from the top, keeping the left edges flush.

5  Attach the specified photos (photos 1-3) to the appropriate areas, centering them on the mats.

## Liquid Glass on Vellum

**STEP 1**  Stamp your image on vellum using VersaMark® ink. Mix Liquid Glass with Re-inker to create desired shade.

**STEP 2**  Paint inked mixture over image with a dry brush until achieving desired thickness. Let dry and cut out using the VersaMark® stamped image as a guide.

**JEANETTE'S TIP**

Add a vellum library pocket to showcase your journaling.

*For full Recipe see index pg. 122*

# Everything in Its Place

### Layout Materials

12" × 12" Base Cardstock (2)
12" × 12" Cardstock (3)
12" × 12" B&T Paper (2)

### Left Page Dimensions

A  6" × 12" (torn diagonally)
B  6" × 8"
C  5" × 12"
D  4½" × 6"

### Right Page Dimensions

E  3" × 12" (2½" × 12" torn)
F  5" × 4½"
G  5" × 12"
H  1" × 6"
I  9" × 6" (4½" × 6" folded)

### Photo Suggestions

1  5" × 7"
2  4" × 5½"
3  3" × 2¼" (4)
4  2¼" × 3" (4)

### Suggested Title

1  1" × 6"

### Suggested Journaling

1  4½" × 4"

**LEFT**

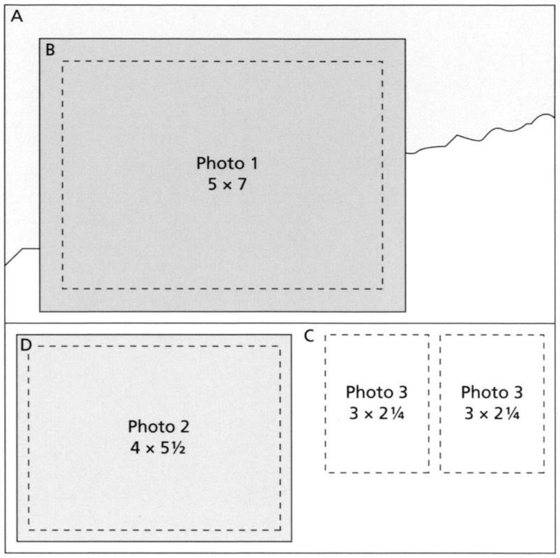

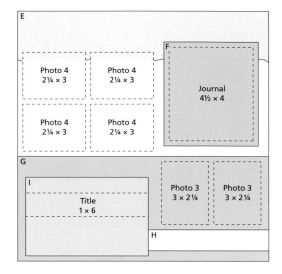

A
B
Photo 1
5 × 7

D
Photo 2
4 × 5½

C
Photo 3
3 × 2¼
Photo 3
3 × 2¼

**RIGHT**

E
Photo 4
2¼ × 3
Photo 4
2¼ × 3
F
Journal
4½ × 4

Photo 4
2¼ × 3
Photo 4
2¼ × 3

G
I
Title
1 × 6
Photo 3
3 × 2¼
Photo 3
3 × 2¼
H

**1** Decoratively tear or cut piece A diagonally as shown in the cutting diagrams.

**2** Using one 12" × 12" cardstock as your base, attach piece A to the top left corner of the page, keeping the edges flush.

**3** Attach piece B to the page, placing it ¾" from the top and left edges.

**4** Attach piece C to the bottom of the page, keeping the edges flush.

**5** Attach piece D, placing it ¼" from the left and bottom edges.

**6** Attach the specified photos (photos 1-3) to the appropriate areas, centering them on the mats.

**1** Decoratively tear or cut approximately ½" from piece E as shown in the cutting diagrams.

**2** Using one 12" × 12" cardstock as your base, attach piece E to the top of the page, keeping the edges flush.

**3** Attach piece F, placing it 1½" from the top and ½" from the right edge of the page.

**4** Attach piece G to the bottom of the page, keeping the edges flush.

**5** Attach piece H to the bottom right corner of the page, placing it ½" from the bottom, keeping the right edges flush.

**6** Cut and fold piece I. Attach it ½" from the left and ¼" from the bottom of the page.

**7** Attach the specified photos (photos 3-4) to the appropriate areas, centering them on the mats.

beautiful

blissful

believe

Ever since I can remember, I have always wanted to be a mom. When we found out I was pregnant, I was so excited, a little scared, a little overwhelmed but mainly excited. Each month, getting closer and closer to my due date, I feel more motherly. Every time you kick, or move, I stop and take a second to cling to that feeling, knowing that it wont last forever. Even though I feel so inadequate and want to do such a great job as a mother, I cant wait for my delivery date, to meet you and hold you in my arms, never to let you go. I already love you so much.

my feelings

baby

*pregnancy*

Timeline

*Cutting Instructions*

**B&T Paper**

C
5 × 12

H 1 × 6

SCRAP

**B&T Paper**

A
6 × 12

E
3 × 12

SCRAP

**Cardstock**

D
4½ × 6

I
9 × 6

SCRAP

**Cardstock***

G
5 × 12

B
6 × 8

SCRAP

**Cardstock***

F
5 × 4½

SCRAP

*Identical papers

55

**WRAP THINGS UP WITH A JAZZY CONCLUSION**

---

*Cutting Instructions*

**B&T Paper**

G
6 × 1½

F
12 × 1½

B
12 × 1½

SCRAP

**Cardstock**

H
6 × 10½

A
6 × 6

E
5 × 5

SCRAP

**Cardstock**

C 1 × 7    I 1 × 5

SCRAP

**Cardstock**

D
6 × 6

SCRAP

# Conclusion Combo

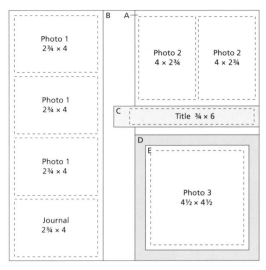

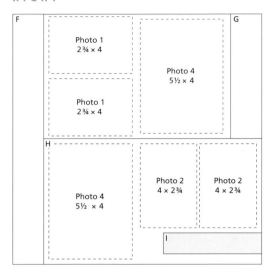

## Layout Materials

12" × 12" Base Cardstock (2)

12" × 12" Cardstock (3)

12" × 12" B&T Paper (1)

## Left Page Dimensions

A  6" × 6"
B  12" × 1½"
C  1" × 7"
D  6" × 6"
E  5" × 5"

## Right Page Dimensions

F  12" × 1½"
G  6" × 1½"
H  6" × 10½"
I  1" × 5"

## Photo Suggestions

1  2¾" × 4" (5)
2  4" × 2¾" (4)
3  4½" × 4½"
4  5½" × 4" (2)

## Suggested Title

1  ¾" × 6"

## Suggested Journaling

1  2¾" × 4"

### Left layout labels

- B  A
- Photo 1  2¾ × 4
- Photo 2  4 × 2¾
- Photo 2  4 × 2¾
- Photo 1  2¾ × 4
- C  Title  ¾ × 6
- D
- E
- Photo 1  2¾ × 4
- Photo 3  4½ × 4½
- Journal  2¾ × 4

### Right layout labels

- F  G
- Photo 1  2¾ × 4
- Photo 4  5½ × 4
- Photo 1  2¾ × 4
- H
- Photo 4  5½ × 4
- Photo 2  4 × 2¾
- Photo 2  4 × 2¾
- I

### Left instructions

1  Using one 12" × 12" cardstock as your base, attach piece A to the top right corner of the page, keeping the edges flush.

2  Attach piece B directly to the left of piece A, keeping the top and bottom edges flush.

3  Attach piece C across pieces A and B, placing it 4½" from the top of the page, keeping the right edges flush.

4  Attach piece D to the bottom right corner of the page, keeping the edges flush.

5  Attach piece E to the center of piece D.

6  Attach the specified photos (photos 1-3) to the appropriate areas, centering them on the mats.

### Right instructions

1  Using one 12" × 12" cardstock as your base, attach piece F to the left side of the page, keeping the edges flush.

2  Attach piece G to the top right corner of the page, keeping the edges flush.

3  Attach piece H to the bottom right corner of the page, keeping the edges flush.

4  Attach piece I to the right side of the page, placing it ½" from the bottom, keeping the right edges flush.

5  Attach the specified photos (photos 1-2 and 4) to the appropriate areas.

## Stamping on Photos with StazOn®

**STEP 1**  Arrange letters in reverse order on an acrylic block; you can look through the block from the other side to check spelling.

**STEP 2**  Press stamp into StazOn® pad, stamp image on photo, and clean stamp immediately. Let dry.

### JEANETTE'S TIP

You may wish to cover your exposed base page with additional papers in order to add even distressing to paper edges. Simply measure exposed space and cut from additional papers.

*For full Recipe see index pg. 123*

# Dialogue

## Layout Materials

12" × 12" Base Cardstock (2)
12" × 12" Cardstock (3)
12" × 12" B&T Paper (3)

## Photo Suggestions

1  4" × 6" (2)
2  2½" × 2½" (3)
3  3" × 3" (2)

## Left Page Dimensions

A  8" × 3"
B  8" × 9"
C  5" × 7"
D  4" × 4" (torn diagonally)
E  1½" × 12" (1" × 12" torn)
F  5½" × 3½" (2)
    (5" × 3½" torn)

## Suggested Title

1  2½" × 6"

## Suggested Journaling

1  3" × 3"

## Right Page Dimensions

G  11½" × 12"
H  1½" × 12" (1" × 12" torn)
I   3" × 8"
J  4" × 4" (torn diagonally)
K  3" × 3" (torn diagonally)
L  8½" × 6" (8" × 6" torn)
M  5½" × 3½"
    (5" × 3½" torn)
N  6" × 8½" (6" × 8" torn)
O  5" × 7"

**JEANETTE'S TIP**

Your title doesn't have to stay straight—curve it, bend it, or let a letter drop off one end to reflect the look of your page.

**Stippling.** *For full Recipe and Technique see index pg. 123*

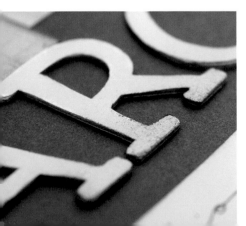

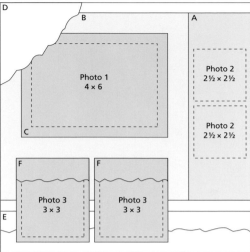

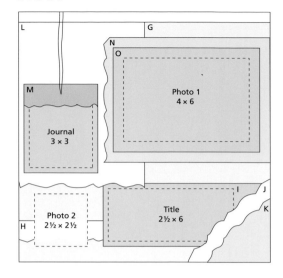

**1** Decoratively tear or cut approximately ½" from pieces E, and F (2) as shown in the cutting diagrams. Decoratively tear or cut piece D (J) in half diagonally as shown in cutting diagrams.

**2** Using one 12" × 12" cardstock as your base, attach piece A to the right side of the page, placing it ½" from the top, keeping the right edges flush.

**3** Attach piece B to the left side of the page, placing it ½" from the top, keeping the left edges flush.

**4** Attach piece C to piece B, placing it 1" from the top and left edges of piece B.

**5** Attach D to the top left corner of the page, adhering only on the top and left edges in order to place a photo underneath.

**6** Attach piece E, placing it 1" from the bottom of the page, keeping the side edges flush.

**7** Leaving a 4" base, fold the torn top edge of both pieces F over approximately 1".

**8** Attach the two pieces F to the bottom of the page, placing them ¾" from the left edge, ½" from the bottom, and ¼" from each other.

**9** Attach the specified photos (photos 1-3) to the appropriate areas, centering them on the mats.

**1** Decoratively tear or cut approximately ½" from pieces H, L, M, and N as shown in the cutting diagrams. Decoratively tear or cut pieces J (D), and K in half diagonally as shown in the cutting diagrams.

**2** Using one 12" × 12" cardstock as your base, attach piece G to the page, placing it ½" from the top, keeping the edges flush.

**3** Attach piece H across the bottom of piece G, placing it 1" from the bottom, keeping the side edges flush.

**4** Attach piece I to the bottom right corner of the page, placing it ¾" from the bottom, keeping the right edges flush.

**5** Attach piece J to the bottom right corner of the page, keeping the edges flush.

**6** Attach piece K to the bottom right corner of piece J, keeping the edges flush.

**7** Attach piece L to the left side of the page, placing it ½" from the top, keeping the left edges flush.

**8** Leaving a 4" base, fold the torn top edge of piece M over approximately 1". Attach piece M to the page, placing it 3½" from the top and ¼" from the left edge.

**9** Attach an 8" piece of fiber to piece M as illustrated if desired.

**10** Attach piece N to the right side of the page, placing it 1¼" from the top, keeping the right edges flush.

**11** Attach piece O to the center of piece N.

**12** Attach the specified photos (photos 1-2) to the appropriate areas, centering them on the mats.

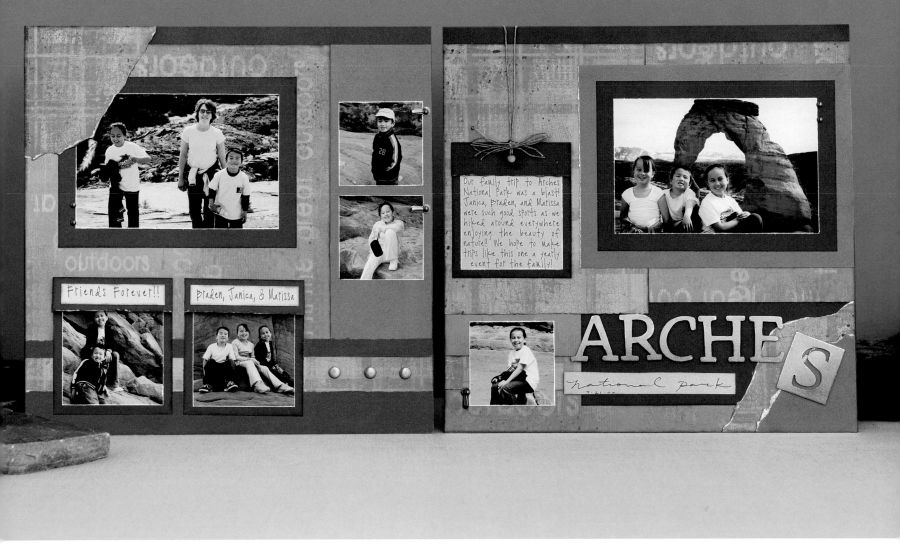

*Friends Forever!!*

*Braden, Janica, & Marissa*

Our family trip to Arches National Park was a blast! Janica, Braden, and Marissa were such good sports as we hiked around everywhere enjoying the beauty of nature!! We hope to make trips like this one a yearly event for the family!

ARCHES

*national park*

## Cutting Instructions

**B&T Paper**

- E 1½ × 12
- H 1½ × 12
- D
- 4 × 4
- J
- L 8½ × 6
- SCRAP

**B&T Paper***

- G 11½ × 12
- SCRAP

**B&T Paper***

- B 8 × 9
- SCRAP

**Cardstock**

- A 8 × 3
- N 6 × 8½
- K 3 × 3
- SCRAP

**Cardstock****

- C 5 × 7
- F 5½ × 3½
- O 5 × 7
- F 5½ × 3½
- SCRAP

**Cardstock****

- I 3 × 8
- M 5½ × 3½
- SCRAP

*Identical papers **Identical papers

VIBRANT, FESTIVE, AND BEAUTIFUL, AS A FIESTA SHOULD BE

- stood in 43 lines
- used 10 fast passes
- ate 7 caramel apples
- bought 5 pairs of Mickey Mouse ears
- hugged 9 princesses
- rode Pirates of the Caribbean 4 times
- had too much fun to quantify

................... *Cutting Instructions* ...................

**B&T Paper**

D
12 × 6

H
6 × 12

**B&T Paper***

G
9 × 12

SCRAP

**B&T Paper***

A
9 × 7

E
5 × 4

K 1 × 3

I
3 × 6½

SCRAP

**Cardstock**

M
2½ × 4½

C 1 × 3

F
2¼ × 3

J
3 × 2¼

SCRAP

**Cardstock**

B
½ × 7

L
7 × 5

SCRAP

*Identical papers

60

# Fiesta

## Layout Materials

12" × 12" Base
Cardstock (2)

12" × 12"
Cardstock (2)

12" × 12" B&T
Paper (3)

## Left Page Dimensions

A  9" × 7"
   (8½" × 7" torn)

B  ½" × 7"

C  1" × 3"

D  12" × 6"
   (12" × 5½" torn)

E  5" × 4"

F  2¼" × 3" oval

## Right Page Dimensions

G  9" × 12"
   (8½" × 12" torn)

H  6" × 12"
   (5½" × 12" torn)

I  3" × 6½"
   (2½" × 6" torn)

J  3" × 2¼" oval

K  1" × 3"

L  7" × 5"

M  2½" × 4½"

## Photo Suggestions

1  5" × 3½" (3)

2  6" × 4"

## Suggested Title

1  1" × 5½"

## Suggested Journaling

1  2" × 4"

**LEFT**

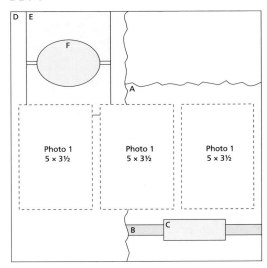

**RIGHT**

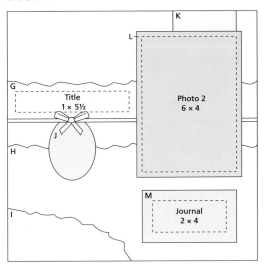

### LEFT

1  Decoratively tear or cut no more than ½" from pieces A and D as shown in the cutting diagrams.

2  Using one 12" × 12" cardstock as your base, attach piece A to the bottom right corner of the page, keeping the edges flush.

3  Attach piece B to piece A, placing it 1¼" from the bottom edge of the page, keeping the right edges flush.

4  Attach piece C to the center of piece B.

5  Attach piece D to the left side of the page, keeping the edges flush.

6  Attach piece E to the top of piece D, centered side-to-side, keeping the top edges flush.

7  Attach piece F to the center of piece E, using ribbon to secure from the back, if desired.

8  Attach the specified photos (photos 1) to the appropriate areas.

### RIGHT

1  Decoratively tear or cut no more than ½" from pieces G, H, and I as shown in the cutting diagrams.

2  Using one 12" × 12" cardstock as your base, attach piece G to the bottom of the page, keeping the edges flush.

3  Attach piece H to the bottom of piece G, keeping the edges flush.

4  Attach piece I to the bottom of piece H, keeping the left and bottom edges flush.

5  Attach piece J by tying a ribbon around the page and securing with a bow, if desired.

6  Attach piece K, placing it 1" from the right edge, keeping the top edges flush.

7  Attach piece L, placing it 1" from the top and ¾" from the right edge of the page.

8  Attach piece M below piece L, placing it 1" from the bottom and right edges of the page.

9  Attach the specified photo (photo 2) to the appropriate area, centering it on the mat.

## Empressing with Metal-rimmed Tags

**STEP 1**  Place a metal-rimmed tag under cardstock; run empressor tool around the outside of the tag to create a raised edge.

**STEP 2**  Sand and/or sponge daub the raised edge to create a highlight.

### JEANETTE'S TIP

Even if you don't love your handwriting, incorporate small pieces of your handwriting into your layouts to represent a little bit of yourself!

*For full Recipe see index pg. 123*

# Fantastic Five

## Layout Materials

12" × 12" Base Cardstock (2)
12" × 12" Cardstock (3)
12" × 12" B&T Paper (2)

## Left Page Dimensions

A  12" × 1 ½"
B  12" × ½"
C  12" × ½"
D  11" × 9"
E  2" × 9"
F  8" × 6"
G  2 ½" × 2 ½" (2)

## Right Page Dimensions

H  1" × 12"
I  2 ½" × 12"
J  4 ½" × 6 ½"
K  6" × 6"
L  4 ½" × 4 ½"
M  6" × 6"
N  4 ½" × 4 ½"

## Photo Suggestions

1  2" × 2" (2)
2  7" × 5"
3  4" × 6"
4  4" × 4"

## Suggested Title

1  2" × 4"

## Suggested Journaling

1  4" × 4"

## JEANETTE'S TIP

Pop specific elements off your page with foam squares. They also add pleasing depth when layering letters from various fonts in a title.

**Sponge Daubing.** *For full Recipe and Technique see index pg. 123*

### LEFT

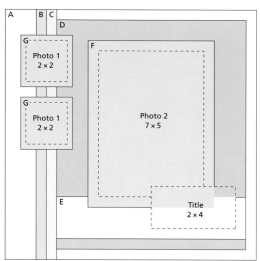

1  Using one 12" × 12" cardstock as your base, attach piece A to the left side of the page, keeping the edges flush.

2  Attach piece B to the page, placing it directly to the right of piece A, keeping the edges flush.

3  Attach piece C to the page, placing it directly to the right of piece B, keeping the edges flush.

4  Attach piece D to the page, placing it ½" from the top, keeping the left edge flush with the right edge of piece C.

5  Attach piece E to the bottom of piece D, placing it ½" from the bottom, keeping the right edges flush.

6  Attach piece F to pieces D and E, placing it 1½" from the top and 2" from the right side of the page.

7  Attach the two piece G squares to the top of the page, placing them ¾" from the right, 1¼" from the top, and ½" from each other.

8  Attach the specified photos (photos 1-2) to the appropriate areas, centering them on the mats.

### RIGHT

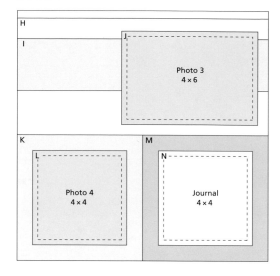

1  Using one 12" × 12" cardstock as your base, attach piece H to the page ½" from the top, keeping the side edges flush.

2  Attach piece I to the page, placing it directly below piece H, keeping the side edges flush.

3  Attach piece J to the page, placing it 1" from the top and ½" from the right edge.

4  Attach piece K to the bottom left corner of the page, keeping the edges flush.

5  Attach piece L to the center of piece K.

6  Attach piece M to the bottom right corner of the page, keeping the edges flush.

7  Attach piece N to the center of piece M.

8  Attach the specified photos (photos 3-4) to the appropriate areas, centering them on the mats.

My family is the most important thing in my life. When I was a child I had always wanted to be a mom but I never knew the joys it would truly bring. I have learned that it is not enough to plan to be the perfect mother some day, but that it is most important to be best mother that I can be right now.

*Johnson Family 2007*

TOGETHER

WE CAN DO ANYTHING

## Cutting Instructions

**B&T Paper**

- A 12 × 1½
- H 1 × 12
- E 2 × 9
- N 4½ × 4½
- SCRAP

**B&T Paper**

- I 2½ × 12
- C 12 × ½
- K 6 × 6
- SCRAP

**Cardstock**

- J 4½ × 6½
- F 8 × 6
- L 4½ × 4½
- B 12 × ½
- G 2½ × 2½
- SCRAP

**Cardstock***

- M 6 × 6
- SCRAP

**Cardstock***

- D 11 × 9
- SCRAP

*Identical papers

63

Pumpkin Patch Days

It was one of those perfect English autumnal days that occur more frequently in memory than in life.  ~P.D. James

**TURN UP THE TEMPO ON YOUR LAYOUTS WITH THIS EASY DESIGN**

.................... *Cutting Instructions* ....................

**B&T Paper**

| A 12 × 3 |
| G 2½ × 12 |
| C 2½ × 7 |
| SCRAP |

**B&T Paper**

| H 4 × 12 |
| D 4 × 4 |
| SCRAP |

**Cardstock**

| B 12 × 2 |
| E 9 × 7 |
| L 1 × 2½ |
| F 1 × 2½ |
| SCRAP |

**Cardstock**

| K 4 × 12 |
| J 4½ × 6½ | I 4½ × 3 |
| SCRAP |

64

# Up the Tempo

**LEFT**

A | B
E

F | Title
F | Title
F | Title

Photo 1
8 × 6

D

C

**RIGHT**

L

K

Photo 2
3½ × 3½ | Photo 2
3½ × 3½ | Photo 2
3½ × 3½

H

I
Journal
4 × 2½

J
Photo 3
4 × 6

G

## Layout Materials

12" × 12" Base
Cardstock (2)

12" × 12"
Cardstock (2)

12" × 12" B&T
Paper (2)

## Left Page Dimensions

A  12" × 3"
B  12" × 2"
C  2½" × 7"
D  4" × 4"
E  9" × 7"
F  1" × 2½" (3)

## Right Page Dimensions

G  2½" × 12"
H  4" × 12"
I  4½" × 3"
J  4½" × 6½"
K  4" × 12"
L  1" × 2½"

## Photo Suggestions

1  8" × 6"
2  3½" × 3½" (3)
3  4" × 6"

## Suggested Title

1  ½" × 2" (3)

## Suggested Journaling

1  4" × 2½"

### LEFT

1  Using one 12" × 12" cardstock as your base, attach piece A to the left side of the page, keeping the edges flush.

2  Attach piece B directly to the right of piece A, keeping the edges flush.

3  Attach piece C to the bottom right corner of the page, keeping the edges flush.

4  Attach piece D directly above piece C, keeping the right edges flush.

5  Attach piece E, placing it 1" from the top and left edges of the page.

6  Attach the three pieces F, placing them 1½" from the top of the page and ¼" from each other, keeping the right edges flush.

7  Attach the specified photo (photo 1) to the appropriate area, centering it on the mat.

### RIGHT

1  Using one 12" × 12" cardstock as your base, attach piece G to the bottom of the page, keeping the edges flush.

2  Attach piece H directly above piece G, keeping the edges flush.

3  Attach piece I, placing it 1" from the left and bottom edges of the page.

4  Attach piece J, placing it 1" from the right and bottom edges of the page.

5  Attach piece K, placing it 1½" from the top of the page, keeping the edges flush.

6  Attach piece L, placing it ¼" from the top of the page, keeping the right edges flush.

7  Attach the specified photos (photos 2-3) to the appropriate areas, centering them on the mats.

**STEP 1**  Cut out each pocket in a six-pocket photo storage page, being careful to cut along the center of the crimped line.

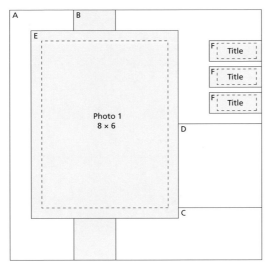

**STEP 2**  Cut out three 4½" × 7½" pieces of cardstock, and attach a photo pocket to each side of each piece. Punch three evenly spaced holes along left hand side and attach mini album to page using three oversized brads.

**JEANETTE'S TIP**

Be creative with your accent pieces. A small strip of paper can translate to a hidden journaling tab.

*For full Recipe see index pg. 123*

# Memoirs Complete

## Layout Materials

12" × 12" Base Cardstock (2)
12" × 12" Cardstock (2)
12" × 12" B&T Paper (2)

### Left Page Dimensions

A  5" × 5"
B  2" × 12"
C  5" × 7"
D  2" × 7"
E  6" × 4"
F  4" × 6"

### Right Page Dimensions

G  4" × 12"
H  1" × 12"
I  7" × 12"
J  2" × 12"
K  6" × 4"

## Photo Suggestions

1  3½" × 5½"
2  3½" × 3½" (4)
3  5½" × 3½" (2)

### Suggested Title

1  2½" × 6½"

### Suggested Journaling

1  4½" × 4½"

**LEFT**

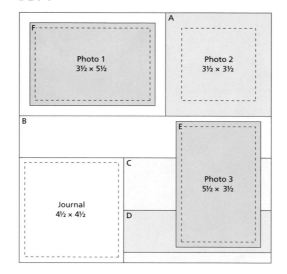

**RIGHT**

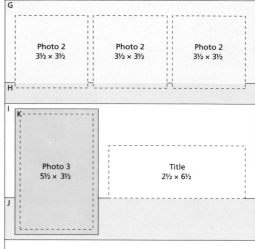

### LEFT

**1** Using one 12" × 12" cardstock as your base, attach piece A to the top right corner of the page, keeping the edges flush.

**2** Attach piece B directly below piece A, keeping the side edges flush.

**3** Attach piece C to the bottom right corner of the page, keeping the edges flush.

**4** Attach piece D to piece C, placing it ½" from the bottom of the page, keeping the right edges flush.

**5** Attach piece E, placing it ½" from the right edge and ¾" from the bottom of the page.

**6** Attach piece F to the top left corner of the page, placing it ½" from the top and left edges.

**7** Attach the specified photos (photos 1-3) to the appropriate areas, centering them on the mats.

### RIGHT

**1** Using one 12" × 12" cardstock as your base, attach piece G to the top of the page, keeping the edges flush.

**2** Attach piece H directly below piece G, keeping the side edges flush.

**3** Attach piece I to the bottom of the page, keeping the edges flush.

**4** Attach piece J to piece I, placing it ½" from the bottom of the page, keeping the side edges flush. (If completing the two-page layout, be sure to line up the piece D and J strips across the pages.)

**5** Attach piece K, placing it ½" from the left edge and ¾" from the bottom of the page.

**6** Attach the specified photos (photos 2-3) to the appropriate areas, centering them on the mats.

christmas: UTAH style?

When we first moved to Arizona, I was excited for a snow-free winter, until we had Xander. I wanted him to experience Christmas the way i did growing up in Utah. So, i tried to make his first Christmas as close to a Utah Christmas as possible. of course without the snow! Troy really didn't enjoy seeing his baby boy dressed up in a basket, but once he saw the pictures, he decided that it was okay—

Xander's first Christmas...

More pictures

merry christmas

HoHo HoHo

december 2005

## Cutting Instructions

**B&T Paper**

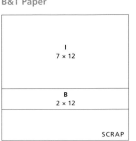

I
7 × 12

B
2 × 12

SCRAP

**B&T Paper**

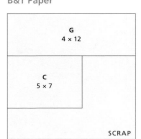

G
4 × 12

C
5 × 7

SCRAP

**Cardstock**

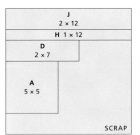

J
2 × 12

H 1 × 12

D
2 × 7

A
5 × 5

SCRAP

**Cardstock**

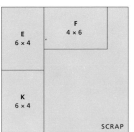

E
6 × 4

F
4 × 6

K
6 × 4

SCRAP

FAMILY

The Hatters

*Cutting Instructions*

**B&T Paper**

C 1 × 12

A
7 × 6

E
7 × 5

H 1 × 7

SCRAP

**B&T Paper**

B
4 × 12

F
4 × 8

SCRAP

**Cardstock**

D
6 × 8

SCRAP

**Cardstock**

G
4 × 4

SCRAP

# Classical Look

## Layout Materials

12" × 12" Base Cardstock (2)

12" × 12" Cardstock (2)

12" × 12" B&T Paper (2)

## Left Page Dimensions

A   7" × 6"
B   4" × 12"
C   1" × 12"
D   6" × 8"

## Right Page Dimensions

E   7" × 5"
F   4" × 8"
G   4" × 4"
H   1" × 7"

## Photo Suggestions

1   2½" × 2½"
2   5" × 7"
3   3" × 3" (3)
4   6" × 3"
5   6" × 4"

## Suggested Title

1   1½" × 5"

## Suggested Journaling

1   3" × 4½"

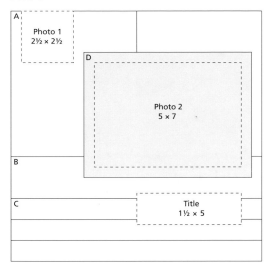

Layout — LEFT: A Photo 1 2½ × 2½; D Photo 2 5 × 7; B; C; Title 1½ × 5

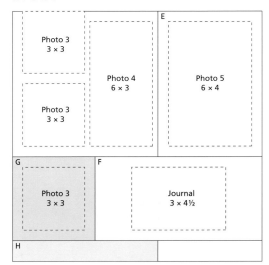

Layout — RIGHT: Photo 3 3 × 3; Photo 4 6 × 3; E Photo 5 6 × 4; Photo 3 3 × 3; G Photo 3 3 × 3; F Journal 3 × 4½; H

### LEFT

1   Using one 12" × 12" cardstock as your base, attach piece A to the top left corner of the page, keeping the edges flush.

2   Attach piece B directly below piece A, keeping the edges flush.

3   Attach piece C across the bottom of piece B, placing it 2" from the bottom of the page, keeping the side edges flush.

4   Attach piece D, placing it 2" from the top and ½" from the right edge of the page.

5   Attach the specified photos (photos 1-2) to the appropriate areas, centering them on the mats.

### RIGHT

1   Using one 12" × 12" cardstock as your base, attach piece E to the top right corner of the page, keeping the edges flush.

2   Attach piece F to the right side of the page, placing it 1" from the bottom, keeping the right edges flush.

3   Attach piece G directly to the left of piece F, keeping the edges flush.

4   Attach piece H to the bottom left corner of the page, keeping the edges flush.

5   Attach the specified photos (photos 3-5) to the appropriate areas, centering them on the mats.

## Creating Embossed Embellishments

**STEP 1**   Cover cardstock just larger than stamp size with embossing ink, add embossing powder, and heat; repeat powder and heat four times, moving quickly so as to not allow embossing to cool between each step.

**STEP 2**   Press stamp into hot embossing powder, allow to cool slightly and remove the stamp. When cool and dry, cut around image.

### JEANETTE'S TIP

Carefully trim stamped letters and then mat and trim again for a powerful title statement.

*For full Recipe see index pg. 124*

# Follow the Lead

## Layout Materials

12" × 12" Base Cardstock (2)
12" × 12" Cardstock (1)
12" × 12" B&T Paper (1)

### Left Page Dimensions

A  8" × 4"
B  2" × 6"

### Right Page Dimensions

C  6" × 9"
D  6" × 3"

## Photo Suggestions

1  10" × 8"
2  4" × 4" (4)

### Suggested Title/Journaling

1  5" × 7"

**LEFT**

**RIGHT**

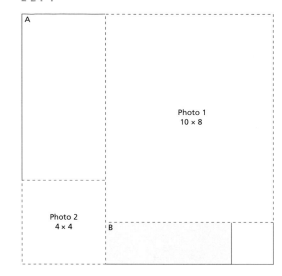

**1** Using one 12" × 12" cardstock as your base, attach piece A to the top left corner of the page, keeping the edges flush.

**2** Attach piece B to the bottom of the page, placing it 2" from the right edge, keeping the bottom edges flush.

**3** Attach the specified photos (photos 1-2) to the appropriate areas.

**1** Using one 12" × 12" cardstock as your base, attach piece C to the top left corner of the page, keeping the edges flush.

**2** Attach piece D to the top right corner of the page, keeping the edges flush.

**3** Attach the specified photos (photos 2) to the appropriate areas.

**JEANETTE'S TIP**

Dress up your layout by using small photos as embellishments.

**Decorative Stitching.** *For full Recipe and Technique see index pg. 124*

SOME LAYOUTS FOLLOW THE LEAD WITH ACCENTS SUPPORTING A LARGE PHOTO

Cutting Instructions

B&T Paper

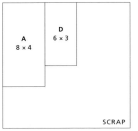

Cardstock

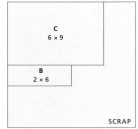

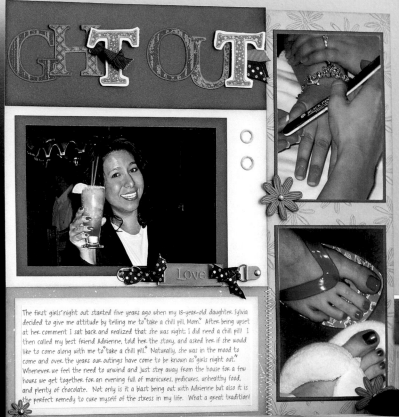

# GIRLS' NIGHT OUT

Love

Joy

The first girls' night out started five years ago when my 13-year-old daughter Sylvia decided to give me attitude by telling me to "take a chill pill, Mom." After being upset at her comment I sat back and realized that she was right; I did need a chill pill! I then called my best friend Adrienne, told her the story, and asked her if she would like to come along with me to "take a chill pill." Naturally, she was in the mood to come and over the years our outings have come to be known as "girls night out." Whenever we feel the need to unwind and just step away from the house for a few hours we get together for an evening full of manicures, pedicures, unhealthy food, and plenty of chocolate. Not only is it a blast being out with Adrienne but also it is the perfect remedy to cure myself of the stress in my life. What a great tradition!

**MAKE IT NICE AND SIMPLE WITH EASY PAGES THAT COME TOGETHER QUICKLY**

.............. *Cutting Instructions* ............................................................................

**B&T Paper**

| | |
|---|---|
| **H** 4 × 8 | **A** 8 × 4 |
| | SCRAP |

**B&T Paper**

| | |
|---|---|
| **J** 12 × 4 | **C** 9 × 8 |
| | SCRAP |

**Cardstock\***

| **D** 7½ × 5½ | **G** 4½ × 6½ |
|---|---|
| | **E** 3 × 3 |
| **F** 3 × 8 | SCRAP |

**Cardstock\***

| **K** 5¼ × 3¾ | **B** 3½ × 3½ |
|---|---|
| | **B** 3½ × 3½ |
| **K** 5¼ × 3¾ | SCRAP |

**Cardstock**

| **I** 3½ × 7½ | |
|---|---|
| | SCRAP |

*\*Identical papers*

# Nice & Simple

## Layout Materials

12" × 12" Base
Cardstock (2)

12" × 12"
Cardstock (3)

12" × 12" B&T
Paper (2)

## Left Page Dimensions

A  8" × 4"
B  3½" × 3½" (2)
C  9" × 8"
D  7½" × 5½"
E  3" × 3"

## Right Page Dimensions

F  3" × 8"
G  4½" × 6½"
H  4" × 8"
I  3½" × 7½"
J  12" × 4"
K  5" × 3½" (2)

## Photo Suggestions

1  3" × 3" (2)
2  7" × 5"
3  4" × 6"
4  4½" × 3" (2)

## Suggested Title

1  2½" × 15½"

## Suggested Journaling

1  3" × 7"

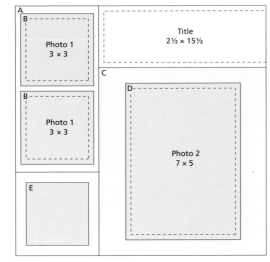

**LEFT diagram:**
A
B — Photo 1 3 × 3
Title 2½ × 15½
C
B — Photo 1 3 × 3
D — Photo 2 7 × 5
E

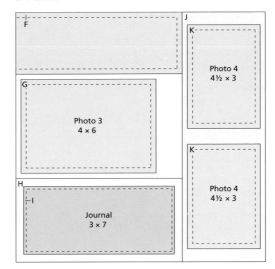

**RIGHT diagram:**
F
G — Photo 3 4 × 6
H
I — Journal 3 × 7
J
K — Photo 4 4½ × 3
K — Photo 4 4½ × 3

### LEFT

1  Using one 12" × 12" cardstock as your base, attach piece A to the top left corner of the page, keeping the edges flush.

2  Attach the two piece B mats to piece A, placing them ¼" from the left edge, ¼" from the top edge, and ⅛" from each other.

3  Attach piece C to the bottom right corner of the page, keeping the edges flush.

4  Attach piece D to piece C, placing it ¾" from the bottom and centered side-to-side.

5  Attach piece E to the page, placing it ½" from the bottom and left edges.

6  Attach the specified photos (photos 1-2) to the appropriate areas, centering them on the mats.

### RIGHT

1  Using one 12" × 12" cardstock as your base, attach piece F to the top left corner of the page, keeping the edges flush.

2  Attach piece G, placing it ¼" below piece F and ¼" from the left edge.

3  Attach piece H to the bottom left corner of the page, keeping the edges flush.

4  Attach piece I to the center of piece H.

5  Attach piece J to the right side of the page, keeping the edges flush.

6  Attach the two piece K mats to piece J, placing them ¼" from the right edge, ½" from the top edge, and ½" from each other.

7  Attach the specified photos (photos 3-4) to the appropriate areas, centering them on the mats.

## Backing Ribbon Slides

**STEP 1** Cut a piece of cardstock the same size as a ribbon slide. Sponge the edges with coordinating ink.

**STEP 2** Attach cardstock to slide with several small dots of Liquid Glass. Anchor with ribbon or other embellishment.

### JEANETTE'S TIP

Create a playful title using an alphabet stamp that includes random background designs.

*For full Recipe see index pg. 124*

# Small Packages

*Layout Materials*

12" × 12" Base Cardstock (2)
12" × 12" Cardstock (1)
12" × 12" B&T Paper (2)

*Left Page Dimensions*

A   12" × 4"
B   12" × 5"
C   1½" × 5"
D   4½" × 6½" (2)

*Right Page Dimensions*

E   12" × 3"
F   1½" × 3"
G   1½" × 12"
H   ½" × 12"

*Photo Suggestions*

1   4" × 6" (2)
2   3" × 3" (10)

*Suggested Title*

1   1" × 4½"

*Suggested Journaling*

1   4½" × 2½"

**LEFT**

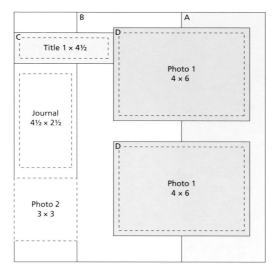

**RIGHT**

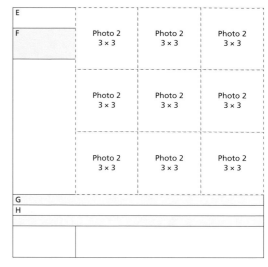

**1**  Using one 12" × 12" cardstock as your base, attach piece A to the right side of the page, keeping the edges flush.

**2**  Attach piece B directly to the left of piece A, keeping the edges flush.

**3**  Attach piece C, placing it 1" from the top, keeping the left edges flush.

**4**  Attach the two pieces D, placing them ¾" from the top and right edges, and 1" from each other.

**5**  Attach the specified photos (photos 1-2) to the appropriate areas, centering them on the mats.

**1**  Using one 12" × 12" cardstock as your base, attach piece E to the left side of the page, keeping the edges flush.

**2**  Attach piece F to piece E, placing it 1" from the top, keeping the edges flush.

**3**  Attach piece G across the page, placing it 1½" from the bottom, keeping the sides flush.

**4**  Attach piece H to the center of piece G, keeping the side edges flush.

**5**  Attach the specified photos (photos 2) to the appropriate areas.

**JEANETTE'S TIP**

Titles and journaling can take a variety of forms, mixing handwriting, stamps, and computer text for many unique looks.

**Holding Ribbon with Hinges.** *For full Recipe and Technique see index pg. 125*

SOMETIMES THE BEST THINGS COME IN SMALL PACKAGES

................. *Cutting Instructions* .................

**B&T Paper**

| B 12 × 5 | E 12 × 3 | H ½ × 12 |
| | | |
| | | SCRAP |

**B&T Paper**

| A 12 × 4 | C 1½ × 5 |
| | F 1½ × 3 |
| | G 1½ × 12 |
| | SCRAP |

**Cardstock**

| D 4½ × 6½ |
| D 4½ × 6½ |
| SCRAP |

blissful

Look at my three handsome little men!

They loved looking tough for the camera.

I think they think that they are pretty hot stuff !

Can I just tell you I cant get enough of Parker, Cooper and Riley.

September 2005

my boys

Riley

parker

cooper

b

......... Cutting Instructions .........

**B&T Paper***

H
5 × 12

A
5 × 7

SCRAP

**B&T Paper***

E
5 × 5½

SCRAP

**B&T Paper**

B
5 × 2½

D
4½ × 4

J
3 × 4

SCRAP

**Cardstock**

F
4 × 2

I
8 × 2

SCRAP

**Cardstock**

G
2½ × 12

C
2½ × 9½

SCRAP

*Identical papers

# Full House

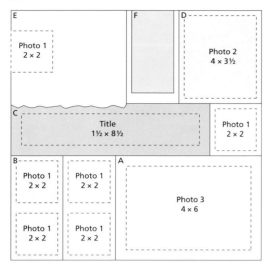

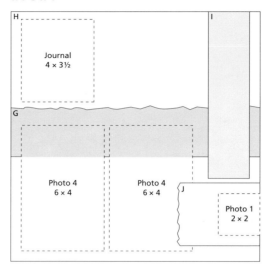

## Layout Materials

12" × 12" Base
Cardstock (2)

12" × 12"
Cardstock (2)

12" × 12" B&T
Paper (3)

## Left Page Dimensions

A  5" × 7"
B  5" × 2½"
C  2½" × 9½"
D  4½" × 4"
E  5" × 5½"
   (4½" × 5½" torn)
F  4" × 2"

## Right Page Dimensions

G  2½" × 12"
H  5" × 12"
   (4½" × 12" torn)
I  8" × 2"
J  3" × 4"
   (3" × 3½" torn)

## Photo Suggestions

1  2" × 2" (7)
2  4" × 3½"
3  4" × 6"
4  6" × 4" (2)

## Suggested Title

1  1½" × 8½"

## Suggested Journaling

1  4" × 3½"

**Layout diagram left:** E, F, D, Photo 1 2 × 2, Photo 2 4 × 3½, C, Title 1½ × 8½, Photo 1 2 × 2, B, A, Photo 1 2 × 2, Photo 1 2 × 2, Photo 3 4 × 6, Photo 1 2 × 2, Photo 1 2 × 2

**Layout diagram right:** H, I, Journal 4 × 3½, G, Photo 4 6 × 4, Photo 4 6 × 4, J, Photo 1 2 × 2

### LEFT

1  Decoratively tear or cut no more than ½" from piece E as shown in the cutting diagrams.

2  Using one 12" × 12" cardstock as your base, attach piece A to the bottom right corner of the page, keeping the edges flush.

3  Attach piece B to the bottom left corner of the page, keeping the edges flush.

4  Attach piece C to the center of the page, directly above pieces A and B keeping the left edges flush.

5  Attach piece D to the top right corner of the page, keeping the edges flush.

6  Attach piece E to the top left corner of the page, keeping the edges flush.

7  Attach piece F to the top of the page, centering it between pieces D and E.

8  Attach the specified photos (photos 1-3) to the appropriate areas, centering them on the mats.

### RIGHT

1  Decoratively tear or cut no more than ½" from pieces H and J as shown in the cutting diagrams.

2  Using one 12" × 12" cardstock as your base, attach piece G across the center of the page, placing it 5" from the bottom, keeping the side edges flush.

3  Attach piece H to the top of the page, keeping the edges flush.

4  Attach piece I to the right side of the page, placing it ½" from the right edge, keeping the top edges flush.

5  Attach piece J to the right side of the page, placing it ¾" from the bottom, keeping the edges flush. Adhering only on the right edge in order to place a photo underneath.

6  Attach the specified photos (photos 1 and 4) to the appropriate areas.

## Tearing and Curling

**STEP 1** Tear cardstock edge to desired size to reveal the white core. Choosing a cardstock with a white core will enhance the technique's effect.

**STEP 2** Roll torn edges up with fingertip.

### JEANETTE'S TIP

Shake up your layout: put a photo in the journaling block and add strips of journaling on photo mats or other empty spaces on the page.

*For full Recipe see index pg. 125*

# Safe & Secure

## Layout Materials

12" × 12" Base Cardstock (2)
12" × 12" Cardstock (4)
12" × 12" B&T Paper (1)

## Left Page Dimensions

A  12" × 8"
B  1½" × 8"
C  4½" × 6½" (2)
D  12" × 4"
E  1½" × 4"
F  3¼" × 3¼"

## Right Page Dimensions

G  12" × 8"
H  8" × 6"
I  7¼" × 5¼"
J  12" × 4"
K  1½" × 4" (2)
L  3¼" × 3¼" (2)
M  1½" × 1¼"
N  1½" × 10¼"

## Photo Suggestions

1  4" × 6" (2)
2  3" × 3" (3)
3  7" × 5"

## Suggested Title/Journaling

1  7½" × 3"

## JEANETTE'S TIP

To add a professional look to a layout, print titles on transparencies to flow over design elements.

**Scissor Distressing.** *For full Recipe and Technique see index pg. 125*

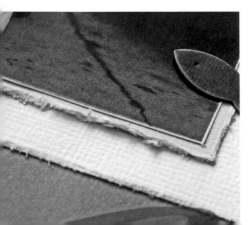

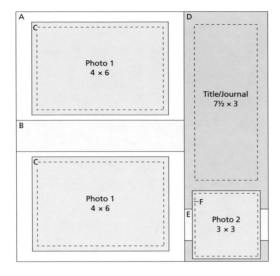

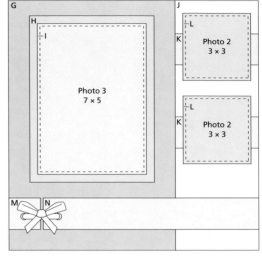

1  Using one 12" × 12" cardstock as your base, attach piece A to the left side of the page, keeping the edges flush.

2  Attach piece B across the center of piece A, placing it 5¼" from the top of the page, keeping the left edges flush.

3  Attach one piece C to the top of piece A, placing it ½" from the top and ¾" from the left edge of the page.

4  Attach remaining piece C to the bottom of piece A, placing it ½" from the bottom and ¾" from the left edge of the page.

5  Attach piece D to the right side of the page, keeping the edges flush.

6  Attach piece E to the bottom of piece D, placing it 1" from the bottom of the page, keeping the side edges flush.

7  Attach piece F centered over piece E, placing it ¼" from the bottom of the page.

8  Attach the specified photos (photos 1-2) to the appropriate areas, centering them on the mats.

1  Using one 12" × 12" cardstock as your base, attach piece G to the left side of the page, keeping the edges flush.

2  Attach piece H, placing it ¾" from the top and 1" from the left edge of the page.

3  Attach piece I in the center of piece H.

4  Attach piece J to the right side of the page, keeping the edges flush.

5  Attach the two pieces K to piece J, placing them 1½" from the top and 2½" from each other, keeping the right edges flush.

6  Attach the two pieces L centered over the two pieces K.

7  Attach piece M to the left side of the page, placing it 1" from the bottom. (If completing the two-page layout, be sure to line up the piece E and M strips across the pages.)

8  Attach piece N to the right side of the page, placing it 1" from the bottom.

9  Using a piece of ribbon, tie pieces M and N together as shown if desired.

10  Attach the specified photos (photos 2-3) to the appropriate areas, centering them on the mats.

PROTECT YOUR PRECIOUS MOMENTS WITH THIS HARMONIOUS MEDLEY

Mr. & Mrs. Ryskamp
"when you realize you've met the person that you want to spend the rest of your life with, you want the rest of your life to start as soon as possible."
I WILL LOVE YOU today, tomorrow,
always
JORDAN & KATELYN
08.19.05

Cutting Instructions

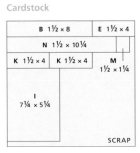

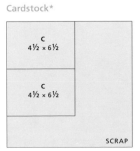

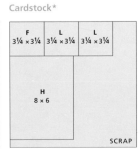

B&T Paper
A 12 × 8
J 12 × 4
Cardstock
B 1½ × 8
E 1½ × 4
N 1½ × 10¼
K 1½ × 4
K 1½ × 4
M 1½ × 1¼
I 7¼ × 5¼
SCRAP
Cardstock*
C 4½ × 6½
C 4½ × 6½
SCRAP
Cardstock*
F 3¼ × 3¼
L 3¼ × 3¼
L 3¼ × 3¼
H 8 × 6
SCRAP
Cardstock
D 12 × 4
G 12 × 8
SCRAP

*Identical papers

FISHIN

If people concentrated on the really important things
in life, there'd be a shortage of fishing poles. ~Doug Larson
May the holes in your net be no larger than the fish in it. ~Irish Blessing
Bragging may not bring happiness, but no man having caught
a large fish goes home through an alley. ~Author Unknown
Nothing makes a fish bigger than almost being caught. ~Author Unknown

**EXPRESSION OF INTENSE ENTHUSIASM IS EMBODIED IN EVERY PHOTO**

......................... *Cutting Instructions* .........................................................................

B&T Paper

| A<br>6 × 3½ | D<br>6 × 3½ |
| --- | --- |

C
2 × 5

F 1½ × 5

SCRAP

B&T Paper

E
3 × 9

B
3 × 7

SCRAP

80

# Rhapsody

**Relief Sanding**

*Layout Materials*

12" × 12" Base
Cardstock (2)

12" × 12" B&T
Paper (2)

*Left Page
Dimensions*

A  6" × 3½"
B  3" × 7"
C  2" × 5"

*Right Page
Dimensions*

D  6" × 3½"
E  3" × 9"
F  1½" × 5"

*Photo
Suggestions*

1  5½" × 3" (5)
2  7" × 5"
3  3" × 3" (2)
4  5" × 7"

*Suggested Title*

1  2" × 6"

*Suggested
Journaling*

1  2" × 8"

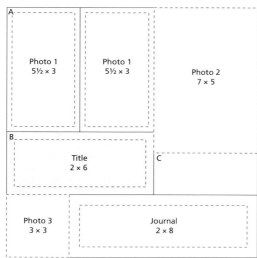

Photo 1 5½ × 3
Photo 1 5½ × 3
Photo 2 7 × 5
Title 2 × 6
C
Photo 3 3 × 3
Journal 2 × 8

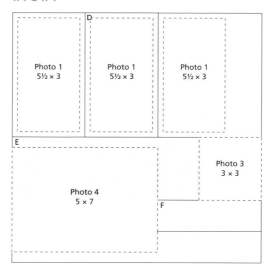

Photo 1 5½ × 3
Photo 1 5½ × 3
Photo 1 5½ × 3
E
Photo 3 3 × 3
Photo 4 5 × 7
F

**STEP 1** Choose a distinctive but thin shape such as a spiral clip.

**STEP 2** Place shape under cardstock and sand lightly to bring out the empression in the white core.

**1** Using one 12" × 12" cardstock as your base, attach piece A to the top left corner of the page, keeping the edges flush.

**2** Attach piece B directly below piece A, keeping the edges flush.

**3** Attach piece C to the right side of the page, placing it 3" from the bottom.

**4** Attach the specified photos (photos 1-3) to the appropriate areas, centering them on the mats.

**1** Using one 12" × 12" cardstock as your base, attach piece D to the top of the page, placing it 3½" from the left edge, keeping the top edges flush.

**2** Attach piece E directly below piece D, keeping the left edges flush.

**3** Attach piece F to the right side of the page, placing it 1½" from the bottom, keeping the right edges flush.

**4** Attach the specified photos (photos 1, 3, and 4) to the appropriate areas, centering them on the mats.

JEANETTE'S TIP

Create embellishments that match the theme of your photos

*For full Recipe see index pg. 125*

# Bits & Pieces

## Layout Materials

12 × 12" Base Cardstock (2)
12" × 12" Cardstock (1)
12" × 12" B&T Paper (4)

## Left Page Dimensions

A  12" × 6"
B  11" × 4"
C  1" × 7"
D  1" × 4"
E  2" × 6"

## Right Page Dimensions

F  4" × 8"
G  2" × 7"
H  8" × 8"
I  7" × 5"
J  3" × 5"
K  1" × 4"
L  1" × 3"

## Photo Suggestions

1  5" × 3" (2)
2  3" × 3" (2)
3  3" × 5"
4  6½" × 4½"
5  2½" × 4½"

## Suggested Title

1  1½" × 5½"

## Suggested Journaling

1  2½" × 5½"

### JEANETTE'S TIP

Journaling can be as big or as small as you want it. Spice up a small journaling block with a large font size.

**Direct-to-Paper.** *For full Recipe and Technique see index pg. 125*

**LEFT**

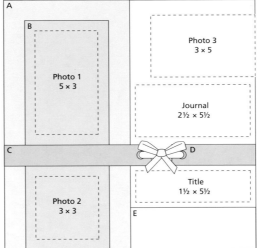

1  Using one 12" × 12" cardstock as your base, attach piece A to the top left corner of the page, keeping the edges flush.

2  Attach piece B to piece A, placing it 1" from the left, keeping the bottom edges flush.

3  Attach piece C, placing it 4" from the bottom, keeping the left edges flush.

4  Attach piece D directly across from piece C, 4" from the bottom, keeping the right edges flush.

5  Using a piece of ribbon, tie pieces C and D together as shown, if desired.

6  Attach piece E to the bottom right corner of the page, keeping the edges flush.

7  Attach the specified photos (photos 1-3) to the appropriate areas, centering them on the mats.

**RIGHT**

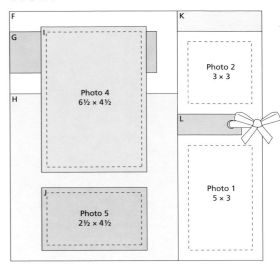

1  Using one 12" × 12" cardstock as your base, attach piece F to the top left corner of the page, keeping the edges flush.

2  Attach piece G to the center of piece F, keeping the left edges flush.

3  Attach piece H to the bottom left corner of the page, keeping the edges flush.

4  Attach piece I to the top of the page, placing it ¾" from the top and 1½" from the left edge.

5  Attach piece J to the bottom of the page, placing it ½" from the bottom and 1½" from the left edge.

6  Attach piece K to the top right corner of the page, keeping the edges flush.

7  Attach piece L, placing it 5" down from the top of the page, keeping the left edge flush against piece H.

8  Using a piece of ribbon, tie piece L to the page as shown, if desired.

9  Attach the specified photos (photos 1, 2, 4, and 5) to the appropriate areas, centering them on the mats.

I can't get enough of this little girl! My sweet Julia is always full of life and energy. She is also very independent. she loves to be silly and laugh and play. And if I'm lucky she will let me take some pictures of her. you can tell by the pouty photo that she was done with taking pictures for the day. which is okay I got some adorable pictures of my little girl.

January 2006

The Many Faces of
**Julia**

**Blos-som** (blŏs'əm) —v. blos'som-y adj.
1.To come into flower; bloom.
2.To develop; flourish.

Blossom

Fab

Blossom

## Cutting Instructions

**B&T Paper**

| F 4 × 8 |
| E 2 × 6 |
| SCRAP |

**B&T Paper***

| K 1 × 4 |
| H 8 × 8 |
| SCRAP |

**B&T Paper***

| A 12 × 6 |
| SCRAP |

**B&T Paper**

| G 2 × 7 |
| C 1 × 7 |
| D 1 × 4 | L 1 × 3 |
| SCRAP |

**Cardstock**

| I 7 × 5 |
| B 11 × 4 |
| J 3 × 5 |
| SCRAP |

*Identical papers

NO MATTER WHAT ELEMENTS YOU USE, A BALANCED RHYTHM BRINGS THE LOOK TOGETHER

*Our life is so rich and full of love. Family is the most important thing and we have an abundance of it. Thank you to my family for always showing love for one another. Chris, Stella, Ebony, Elliot, and Uncle Edward. Summer 2006*

## Cutting Instructions

**B&T Paper**

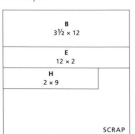

| | |
|---|---|
| **B** 3½ × 12 | |
| **E** 12 × 2 | |
| **H** 2 × 9 | |
| | SCRAP |

**Cardstock\***

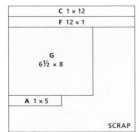

| | |
|---|---|
| **C** 1 × 12 | |
| **F** 12 × 1 | |
| **G** 6½ × 8 | |
| **A** 1 × 5 | SCRAP |

**Cardstock\***

| | |
|---|---|
| **D** 6½ × 6 | |
| | SCRAP |

*\*Identical papers*

# Balanced Rhythm

**Embossed Chipboard Accents**

*Layout Materials*

12" × 12" Base Cardstock (2)

12" × 12" Cardstock (2)

12" × 12" B&T Paper (1)

*Left Page Dimensions*

A   1" × 5"
B   3½" × 12"
C   1" × 12"
D   6½" × 6"

*Right Page Dimensions*

E   12" × 2"
F   12" × 1"
G   6½" × 8"
H   2" × 9"

*Photo Suggestions*

1   2½" × 5" (5)
2   5½" × 5" (2)
3   2½" × 2½" (2)

*Suggested Title*

1   1" × 6"

*Suggested Journaling*

1   5½" × 2"

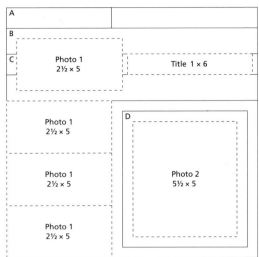

Layout diagram (LEFT page): A, B, C; Photo 1 2½ × 5; Title 1 × 6; Photo 1 2½ × 5; D; Photo 1 2½ × 5; Photo 2 5½ × 5; Photo 1 2½ × 5.

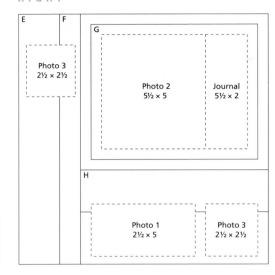

Layout diagram (RIGHT page): E, F; Photo 3 2½ × 2½; G; Photo 2 5½ × 5; Journal 5½ × 2; H; Photo 1 2½ × 5; Photo 3 2½ × 2½.

**1** Using one 12" × 12" cardstock as your base, attach piece A to the top left corner of the page, keeping the edges flush.

**2** Attach piece B directly below piece A, keeping the side edges flush.

**3** Attach piece C to the center of piece B, keeping the side edges flush.

**4** Attach piece D, placing it ½" from the bottom and right edges of the page.

**5** Attach the specified photos (photos 1-2) to the appropriate areas, centering them on the mats.

**1** Using one 12" × 12" cardstock as your base, attach piece E to the left side of the page, keeping the edges flush.

**2** Attach piece F directly to the right of piece E, keeping the edges flush.

**3** Attach piece G, placing it ½" from the top and right edges of the page.

**4** Attach piece H to the right side of the page, placing it 2½" from the bottom, keeping the right edges flush.

**5** Attach the specified photos (photos 1-3) to the appropriate areas.

**STEP 1** Stamp a color image onto a chipboard tag or photo clip.

**STEP 2** Stamp the image again with embossing ink. Add clear embossing powder, tapping off excess, and heat with a heat gun until powder melts.

**JEANETTE'S TIP**

Change your font color to add monochromatic or contrast interest and variety to journaling.

*For full Recipe see index pg. 125*

"FINDING BEAUTY IN THE
EVERYDAY—NOW THAT IS
REAL CREATIVITY."

# Discover

# Staccato

## Layout Materials

12" × 12" Base Cardstock (2)
12" × 12" Cardstock (1)
12" × 12" B&T Paper (3)

### Left Page Dimensions

A  8" × 12"
B  3" × 12"
C  12" × 4"

### Right Page Dimensions

D  8" × 8"
E  8" × 4"
F  3" × 12"
G  4" × 4"

## Photo Suggestions

1  5" × 7"
2  3" × 3" circle (2)
3  5½" × 3½" (3)

### Suggested Title

1  2" × 6½" (2)

### Suggested Journaling

1  1" × 4" (6)
2  1" × 5" (2)
3  1" × 6½" (2)

**Journal Embellishments.** *For full Recipe and Technique see index pg. 126*

**JEANETTE'S TIP**

Try stitching paper pieces and journaling strips to your page.

**LEFT**

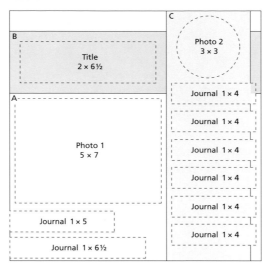

1  Using one 12" × 12" cardstock as your base, attach piece A to the bottom of the page, keeping the edges flush.

2  Attach piece B directly above piece A, keeping the edges flush.

3  Attach piece C, placing it ½" from the right edge, keeping the top and bottom edges flush.

4  Attach the specified photos (photos 1-2) to the appropriate areas.

**RIGHT**

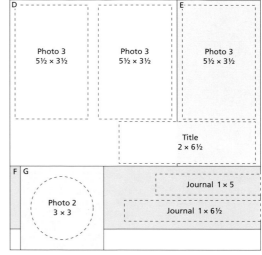

1  Using one 12" × 12" cardstock as your base, attach piece D to the top left corner of the page, keeping the top and left edges flush.

2  Attach piece E to the top right corner of the page, keeping the top and right edges flush.

3  Attach piece F directly below pieces D and E, keeping the side edges flush.

4  Attach piece G to the bottom left corner of the page, placing it ½" from the left edge, keeping the bottom edges flush.

5  Attach the specified photos (photos 2-3) to the appropriate areas.

Why Emma loves

Being with friends

Being with family

Scoring a goal

Having Fun!

Working together as a team

Staying focused

The Excitement of the game!

Hearing her Family and friends cheer her on!

may 2006

Soccer

Emma's soccer Team, the Salmon Dragons!

The Salmon Dragons won the final game of the season!

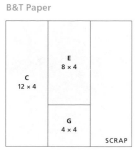

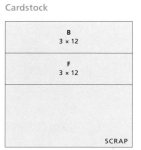

DISTINCTIVE, SHORT, REPEATED PIECES CREATE AN EXCITING PRESENTATION

......... Cutting Instructions .........

**B&T Paper***

| A |
|---|
| 8 × 12 |

SCRAP

**B&T Paper***

| D |
|---|
| 8 × 8 |

SCRAP

**B&T Paper**

| C 12 × 4 | E 8 × 4 |
|---|---|
| | G 4 × 4 |

SCRAP

**Cardstock**

| B 3 × 12 |
|---|
| F 3 × 12 |

SCRAP

*Identical papers

## Cutting Instructions

**B&T Paper**

- B — 5 × 12
- F — 12 × 4
- D — 3½ × 2½
- SCRAP

**B&T Paper**

- G — 6 × 8
- C — 5 × 4
- SCRAP

**Cardstock**

- A — 2 × 12
- E — 4 × 6
- SCRAP

# Personality Presence

**Heightened Letters**

## Layout Materials

12" × 12" Base
Cardstock (2)

12" × 12"
Cardstock (1)

12" × 12" B&T
Paper (2)

## Left Page Dimensions

A  2" × 12"
B  5" × 12"
C  5" × 4"
D  3½" × 2½"
E  4" × 6"

## Right Page Dimensions

F  12" × 4"
G  6" × 8"

## Photo Suggestions

1  4" × 3½" (4)
2  3½" × 5½"
3  5½" × 3½" (4)

## Suggested Title

1  1½" × 11½"

## Suggested Journaling

1  6" × 3"

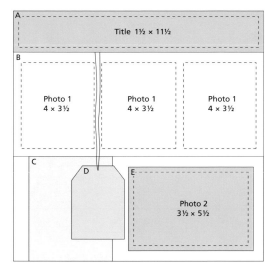

Left layout diagram:
- A — Title 1½ × 11½
- B — Photo 1 4 × 3½ (×3)
- C
- D
- E — Photo 2 3½ × 5½

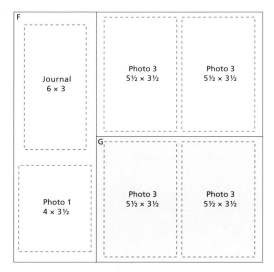

Right layout diagram:
- F — Journal 6 × 3, Photo 1 4 × 3½
- Photo 3 5½ × 3½ (×4)
- G

**1** Using one 12" × 12" cardstock as your base, attach piece A to the top of the page, keeping the edges flush.

**2** Attach piece B directly below piece A keeping the edges flush.

**3** Attach piece C to the bottom of the page, placing it 1" from the left edge, keeping the bottom edges flush.

**4** Cut the top corners of piece D diagonally to create a tag.

**5** Attach piece D to the bottom left corner of the page using a 12" piece of fiber as illustrated if desired.

**6** Attach piece E to the page, placing it ½" from the bottom and right edges.

**7** Attach the specified photos (photos 1-2) to the appropriate areas, centering them on the mats.

**1** Using one 12" × 12" cardstock as your base, attach piece F to the left side of the page, keeping the edges flush.

**2** Attach piece G to the bottom right corner of the page, keeping the edges flush.

**3** Attach the specified photos (photos 1 and 3) to the appropriate areas.

**STEP 1** Stamp or trace a letter image onto cardstock four or five times. Cut them out and glue them on top of each other.

**STEP 2** Use your scissor edge to distress and blend together the layer edges.

**JEANETTE'S TIP**

In journaling, enlarge key words here or there to add visual interest.

*For full Recipe see index pg. 126*

# Stars Above

## Layout Materials

12" × 12" Base Cardstock (2)
12" × 12" Cardstock (1)
12" × 12" B&T Paper (1)

### Left Page Dimensions

A  2" × 4½"
B  1" × 4½"

### Right Page Dimensions

C  2" × 12"
D  1" × 7"
E  2" × 5"

### Photo Suggestions

1  7½" × 7½"
2  2½" × 2½" (5)
3  2½" × 4½"
4  3½" × 5"
5  9" × 7"

### Suggested Title

1  1½" × 11"

### Suggested Journaling

1  4" × 4"

**LEFT**

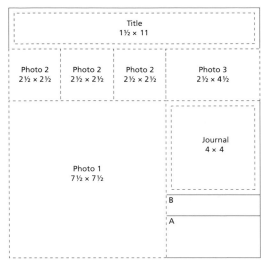

**RIGHT**

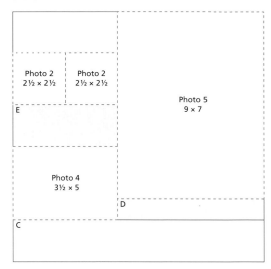

### LEFT

1  Using one 12" × 12" cardstock as your base, attach piece A to the bottom right corner of the page, keeping the edges flush.

2  Attach piece B directly above piece A, keeping the right edges flush.

3  Attach the specified photos (photos 1-3) to the appropriate areas.

### RIGHT

1  Using one 12" × 12" cardstock as your base, attach piece C to the bottom of the page, keeping the edges flush.

2  Attach piece D directly above piece C, keeping the right edges flush.

3  Attach piece E to the left side of the page, placing it 4½" from the top, keeping the left edges flush.

4  Attach the specified photos (photos 2, 4-5) to the appropriate areas.

**JEANETTE'S TIP**

Create a beautiful burned-paper effect by sponging brown ink on the front and back sides of the edges of your paper then rolling the edges forward.

**Faux Metal.** *For full Recipe and Technique see index pg. 126*

## THE WILD WILD WEST

★★★★★★★★★
**WANTED**
$59 THOUSAND & $3 REWARD
FRED "THE BIG CHEESE"
GREEN (BOP)
SOPHIE "THE PIP SQUEAK"
GREENWOOD
THESE OUTLAWS WERE LAST
SEEN AT A JOINT BIRTHDAY
CELEBRATION HELD IN THEIR
HONOR ON JUNE 22, 2006
★★★★★★★★★

SHERIFF
BOP-FRED

................... *Cutting Instructions* ........................................................

**B&T Paper**

| D 1 × 7 | B 1 × 4½ |
|---|---|
| E 2 × 5 | |

SCRAP

**Cardstock**

| C 2 × 12 | |
|---|---|
| A 2 × 4½ | |

SCRAP

.................... Cutting Instructions ....................

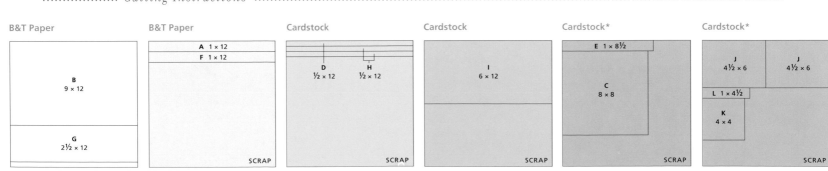

**B&T Paper**

B
9 × 12

G
2½ × 12

**B&T Paper**

A  1 × 12
F  1 × 12

SCRAP

**Cardstock**

D
½ × 12

H
½ × 12

SCRAP

**Cardstock**

I
6 × 12

SCRAP

**Cardstock***

E  1 × 8½

C
8 × 8

SCRAP

**Cardstock***

J
4½ × 6

J
4½ × 6

L  1 × 4½

K
4 × 4

SCRAP

*Identical papers

94

# Subtitles

**Chipboard Shaker Box**

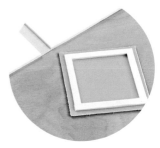

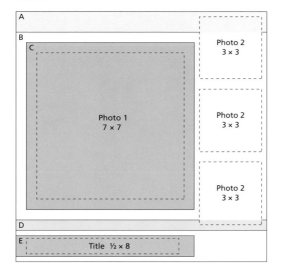

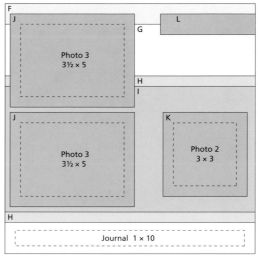

*Layout Materials*

12" × 12" Base
Cardstock (2)

12" × 12"
Cardstock (4)

12" × 12" B&T
Paper (2)

*Left Page
Dimensions*

A   1" × 12"
B   9" × 12"
C   8" × 8"
D   ½" × 12"
E   1" × 8½"

*Right Page
Dimensions*

F   1" × 12"
G   2½" × 12"
H   ½" × 12" (2)
I    6" × 12"
J   4½" × 6" (2)
K   4" × 4"
L   1" × 4½"

*Photo
Suggestions*

1   7" × 7"
2   3" × 3" (4)
3   3½" × 5" (2)

*Suggested Title*

1   ½" × 8"

*Suggested
Journaling*

1   1" × 10"

**STEP 1** Cover a chipboard square with paper. Line edges with foam strips, leaving no open gaps.

**STEP 2** Cover another square with paper, replacing the center with a transparency. Fill bottom square with embellishments and adhere the two squares together using the foam strips.

### Left page instructions

1   Using one 12" × 12" cardstock as your base, attach piece A to the top of the page, keeping the edges flush.

2   Attach piece B directly below piece A, keeping the edges flush.

3   Attach piece C to piece B, placing it ½" from the top and left edges of piece B.

4   Attach piece D directly below piece B, keeping the edges flush.

5   Attach piece E, placing it ¼" from the bottom of the page, keeping the left edges flush.

6   Attach the specified photos (photos 1-2) to the appropriate areas, centering them on the mats.

### Right page instructions

1   Using one 12" × 12" cardstock as your base, attach piece F to the top of the page, keeping the edges flush.

2   Attach piece G directly below piece F, keeping the edges flush.

3   Attach one piece H directly below piece G, keeping the edges flush.

4   Attach piece I directly below piece H, keeping the edges flush.

5   Attach remaining piece H directly below piece I, keeping the edges flush.

6   Attach pieces J to the page placing them ½" from the top, ¼" from the left edge, and ¼" from each other.

7   Attach piece K, placing it ½" from the right edge of the page and 2½" from the bottom.

8   Attach piece L to the right side of the page, placing it ½" from the top, keeping the right edges flush.

9   Attach the specified photos (photos 2-3) to the appropriate areas, centering them on the mats.

**JEANETTE'S TIP**

Add dimension to your layout using small items in your home that support your story.

*For full Recipe see index pg. 126*

**Layout labels (left page):** A, B, C, D, E, Photo 1 7 × 7, Photo 2 3 × 3, Photo 2 3 × 3, Photo 2 3 × 3, Title ½ × 8

**Layout labels (right page):** F, J, G, L, Photo 3 3½ × 5, H, I, J, K, Photo 3 3½ × 5, Photo 2 3 × 3, H, Journal 1 × 10

# Open Forum

## JEANETTE'S TIP

Add variety to your tags, add a tag topper to the photo mat or try mounting one with a mat and one without.

**Denting Oversize Brads.** *For full Recipe and Technique see index pg. 126*

## LEFT

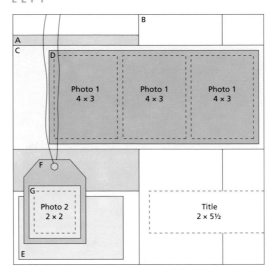

**1** Using one 12" × 12" cardstock as your base, attach piece A to the left side of the page, placing it 1" from the top, keeping the left edges flush.

**2** Attach piece B directly to the right of piece A, keeping the top and bottom edges flush.

**3** Attach piece C to pieces A and B, placing it 1½" from the top of the page, keeping the side edges flush.

**4** Attach piece D to the center of piece C, placing it ¼" from the right edge of the page.

**5** Attach piece E, placing it ¼" from the left and bottom edges.

**6** Cut the top corners of piece F diagonally to create a tag.

**7** Attach piece F, placing it 1" from the bottom and ½" from the left edge of the page.

**8** Attach a 16" piece of fiber to piece F tag as illustrated if desired.

**9** Attach piece G to piece F, placing it ¼" from the side and bottom edges.

**10** Attach the specified photos (photos 1-2) to the appropriate areas, centering them on the mats.

## RIGHT

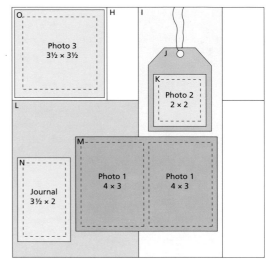

**1** Using one 12" × 12" cardstock as your base, attach piece H to the top right corner of the page, keeping the edges flush.

**2** Attach piece I to the right side of the page, placing it 2" from the right edge, keeping the top and bottom edges flush.

**3** Cut the top corners of piece J diagonally to create a tag.

**4** Attach piece J, placing it 2" from the top and centered from side-to-side on piece I.

**5** Attach a 6" piece of ribbon to piece J tag as illustrated if desired.

**6** Attach piece K to piece J, placing it ¼" from the side and bottom edges.

**7** Attach piece L to the bottom left corner of the page, keeping the edges flush.

**8** Attach piece M, placing it 2¼" from the right edge and 1½" from the bottom edge of the page.

**9** Attach piece N, placing it ¼" from the left edge and ½" from the bottom of the page.

**10** Attach piece O to the upper left corner of the page, placing it ¼" from the top and left edges.

**11** Attach the specified photos (photos 1-3) to the appropriate areas, centering them on the mats.

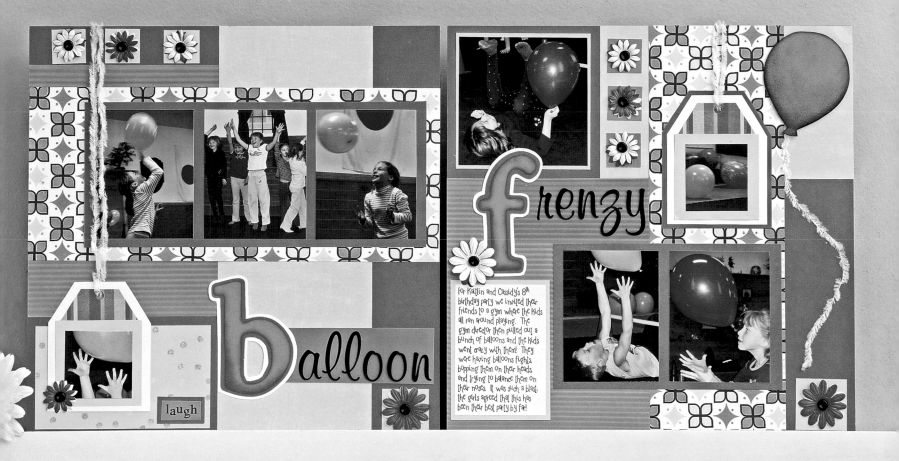

**frenzy**

**balloon**

laugh

For Kaitlin and Cassidy's 8th birthday party we invited their friends to a gym where the kids all ran around playing. The gym director then pulled out a bunch of balloons and the kids went crazy with them! They were having balloon fights, bopping them on their heads, and trying to balance them on their noses. It was such a blast; the girls agreed that this has been their best party by far!

---

*Cutting Instructions*

**B&T Paper**

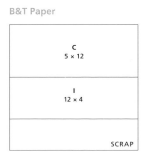

H
4½ × 7½

B
12 × 4½

SCRAP

**B&T Paper**

C
5 × 12

I
12 × 4

SCRAP

**B&T Paper**

O
4 × 4

N
4 × 2½

E
3 × 5

K
2½ × 2½

G
2½ × 2½

SCRAP

**Cardstock**

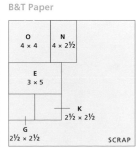

A
7½ × 6

L
7½ × 6

SCRAP

**Cardstock**

F
4 × 3

J
4 × 3

SCRAP

**Cardstock**

D
4½ × 10

M
4½ × 6¾

SCRAP

Cutting Instructions

**B&T Paper**

| A 2½ × 12 |
| D 12 × 5 |
| SCRAP |

**B&T Paper**

| B 2½ × 12 |
| E 2½ × 6 |
| SCRAP |

**Cardstock**

| C 1½ × 12 |
| F 1½ × 6 |
| SCRAP |

# Supporting Cast

*Layout Materials*

12" × 12" Base Cardstock (2)

12" × 12" Cardstock (1)

12" × 12" B&T Paper (2)

*Left Page Dimensions*

A 2½" × 12"
B 2½" × 12"
C 1½" × 12"

*Right Page Dimensions*

D 12" × 5"
E 2½" × 6"
F 1½" × 6"

*Photo Suggestions*

1 4" × 6" (2)
2 2" × 2" (9)
3 4" × 4"
4 6" × 4" (2)

*Suggested Title*

1 1½" × 7½"

*Suggested Journaling*

1 4" × 4"

LEFT

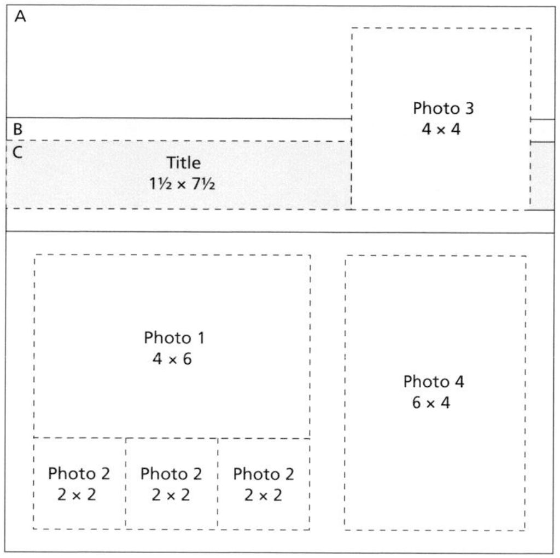

A
B
C
Title
1½ × 7½
Photo 3
4 × 4
Photo 1
4 × 6
Photo 2
2 × 2
Photo 2
2 × 2
Photo 2
2 × 2
Photo 4
6 × 4


1 Using one 12" × 12" cardstock as your base, attach piece A to the top of the page, keeping the edges flush.

2 Attach piece B directly below piece A, keeping the side edges flush.

3 Attach piece C to the center of piece B, keeping the side edges flush.

4 Attach the specified photos (photos 1-4) to the appropriate areas.

RIGHT

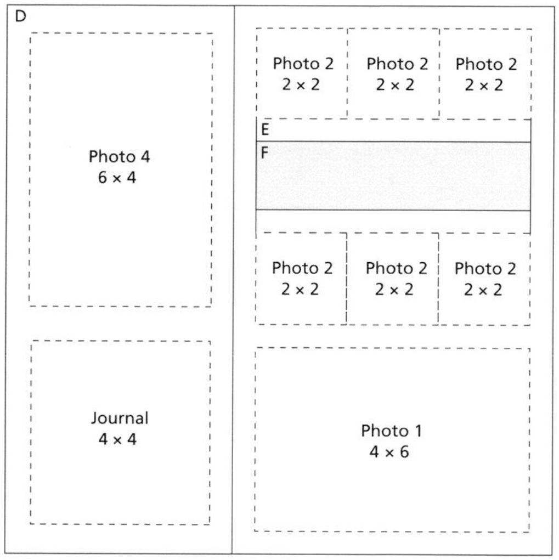

D
Photo 4
6 × 4
Journal
4 × 4
Photo 2
2 × 2
Photo 2
2 × 2
Photo 2
2 × 2
E
F
Photo 2
2 × 2
Photo 2
2 × 2
Photo 2
2 × 2
Photo 1
4 × 6


1 Using one 12" × 12" cardstock as your base, attach piece D to the left side of the page, keeping the edges flush.

2 Attach piece E, placing it 2½" from the top and ½" from the right edge of the page.

3 Attach piece F to the center of piece E, keeping the side edges flush.

4 Attach the specified photos (photos 1, 2, and 4) to the appropriate areas.

**Stamping on Adhesive-backed Vellum**

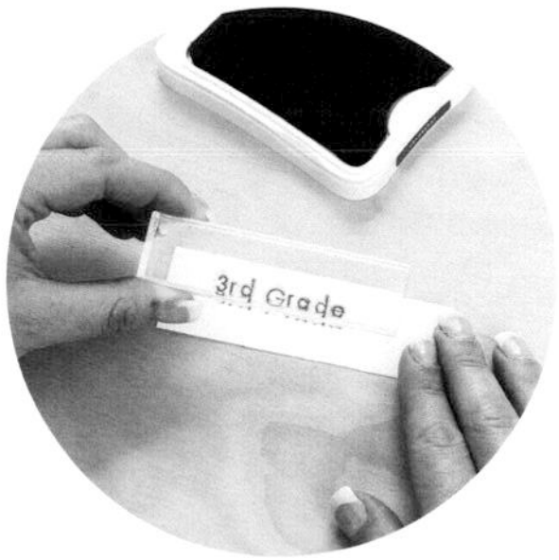

3rd Grade


STEP 1 Gently but firmly stamp image on vellum. Vellum has a smooth surface so use caution to keep your stamp from slipping.

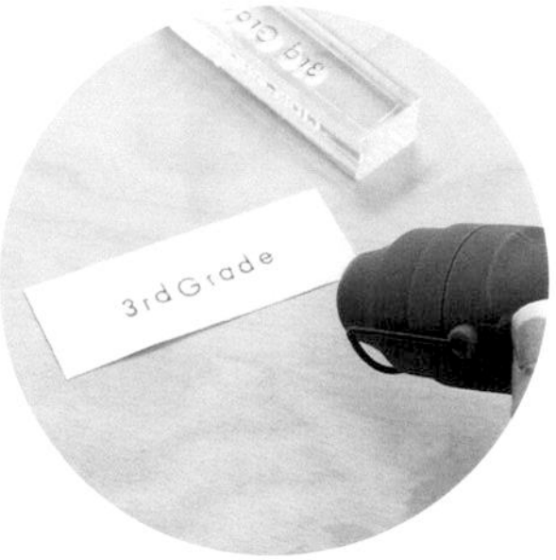

3rd Grade


STEP 2 Set ink with heat gun. Do not overheat or vellum will curl. When dry, attach to your layout.

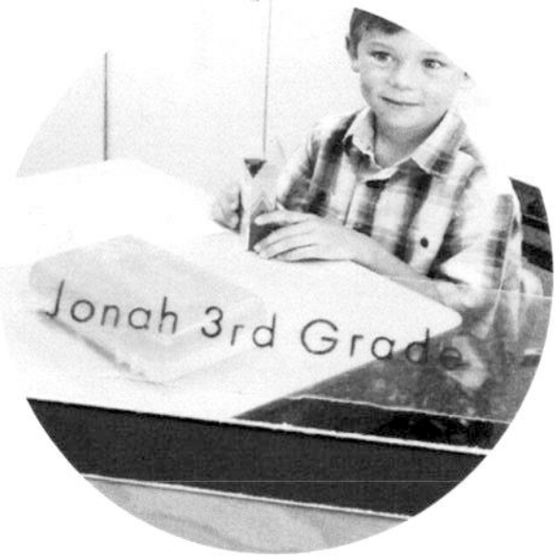

Jonah 3rd Grade


JEANETTE'S TIP

Add interest to journaling by adding subtitles to your journaling block.

*For full Recipe see index pg. 126*

# Thumbnails

## Layout Materials

12" × 12" Base Cardstock (2)
12" × 12" Cardstock (2)
12" × 12" B&T Paper (1)

## Left Page Dimensions

A  2" × 12"
B  1½" × 12"
C  8" × 6"

## Right Page Dimensions

D  5" × 12"
E  2½" × 12"
F  4½" × 12"

## Photo Suggestions

1  7" × 5"
2  2" × 2" (12)
3  3½" × 3½" (3)

## Suggested Title

1  2" × 4"

## Suggested Journaling

1  4" × 4"

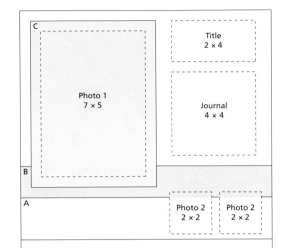

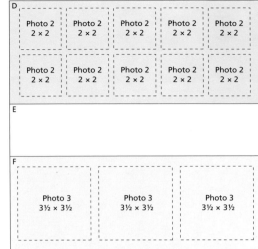

**1** Using one 12" × 12" cardstock as your base, attach piece A to the page, placing it 1" from the bottom, keeping the side edges flush.

**2** Attach piece B directly above piece A, keeping the side edges flush.

**3** Attach piece C to the top left side of the page, placing it ½" from the top and left edges.

**4** Attach the specified photos (photos 1-2) to the appropriate areas, centering them on the mats.

**1** Using one 12" × 12" cardstock as your base, attach piece D to the top of the page, keeping the edges flush.

**2** Attach piece E directly below piece D, keeping the edges flush.

**3** Attach piece F to the bottom of the page, keeping the edges flush.

**4** Attach the specified photos (photos 2-3) to the appropriate areas.

---

**JEANETTE'S TIP**

Walk through a series of events by journaling in chronological order.

**Stamping on Metal.** *For full Recipe and Technique see index pg. 127*

**FILL UP A PAGE WITH NUMEROUS SMALL THUMBNAIL PHOTOS**

*Cutting Instructions*

**B&T Paper**

| E |
|---|
| 2½ × 12 |

| A |
|---|
| 2 × 12 |

SCRAP

**Cardstock**

| F |
|---|
| 4½ × 12 |

| C |
|---|
| 8 × 6 |

SCRAP

**Cardstock**

| D |
|---|
| 5 × 12 |

| B 1½ × 12 |
|---|

SCRAP

### The 7th Annual Watson Family Easter Picnic

Every year the family gets together for an Easter picnic. Mom and Dad like to do it up really big for their grandchildren. They have everything from dyeing eggs to hunting hidden eggs to the Easter Bunny himself making an appearance. Most of the kids love it, including little McKenzie, but unfortunately it was still a little too different and scary for little Ethan!!

some **BUNNY** loves you

APRIL 2006

MANY ELEMENTS ELICIT A DOUBLE TAKE FOR SIMILAR SIZING AND PLACEMENT

---

*Cutting Instructions*

**B&T Paper**

| | |
|---|---|
| B 12 × 6 | F 6 × 12 |
| | SCRAP |

**Cardstock**

| | I 3 × 9 |
|---|---|
| A 12 × 3 | C 8 × 3 |
| | SCRAP |

**Cardstock***

| | |
|---|---|
| H 6½ × 4½ | H 6½ × 4½ |
| | D ½ × 5 |
| J 3 × 3 | SCRAP |
| G 12 × ½ | |

**Cardstock***

| E 4½ × 6½ |
|---|
| E 4½ × 6½ |
| SCRAP |

*Identical papers

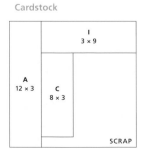

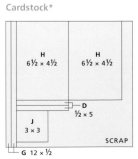

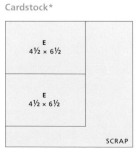

# Double Take

**Inked Flower Photo Corners**

*Layout Materials*

12" × 12" Base
Cardstock (2)

12" × 12"
Cardstock (3)

12" × 12" B&T
Paper (1)

*Left Page
Dimensions*

A   12" × 3"
B   12" × 6"
C   8" × 3"
D   ½" × 5" (2)
E   4½" × 6½" (2)

*Right Page
Dimensions*

F   6" × 12"
G   12" × ½" (2)
H   6½" × 4½" (2)
I   3" × 9"
J   3" × 3"

*Photo
Suggestions*

1   4" × 6" (2)
2   6" × 4" (2)
3   2½" × 2½"

*Suggested Title*

1   2½" × 8½"

*Suggested
Journaling*

1   5½" × 2½"

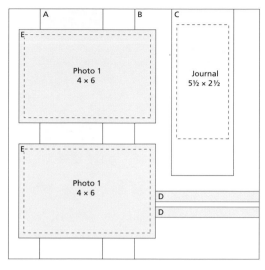

Diagram labels: A, B, C; E — Photo 1 4 × 6; Journal 5½ × 2½; E — Photo 1 4 × 6; D, D

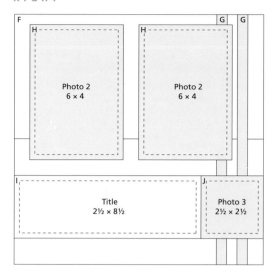

Diagram labels: F, H, H, G, G; Photo 2 6 × 4; Photo 2 6 × 4; I — Title 2½ × 8½; J — Photo 3 2½ × 2½

## LEFT

1   Using one 12" × 12" cardstock as your base, attach piece A, placing it 1½" from the left edge, keeping the top and bottom edges flush.

2   Attach piece B to the right side of the page, keeping the edges flush.

3   Attach piece C to piece B, placing it 1¼" from the right edge, keeping the top edges flush.

4   Attach the two pieces D to the bottom right corner of the page, placing them 2" from the bottom, and ¼" from each other, keeping the right edges flush.

5   Attach one piece E, placing it 1" from the top of the page and ½" from the left edge. Attach the remaining piece E, placing it 1" from the bottom of the page and ½" from the left edge.

6   Attach the specified photos (photos 1) to the appropriate areas, centering them on the mats.

## RIGHT

1   Using one 12" × 12" cardstock as your base, attach piece F to the top of the page, keeping the edges flush.

2   Attach the two pieces G down the right side of the page, placing them ¾" from the right edge and ½" from each other, keeping the top and bottom edges flush.

3   Attach the two pieces H, placing them ½" from the top of the page, ¾" from the left edge, and ¾" from each other.

4   Attach piece I, placing it 1¼" from the bottom of the page, keeping the left edges flush.

5   Attach piece J to the right side of the page, placing it 1¼" from the bottom, keeping the right edges flush.

6   Attach the specified photos (photos 2-3) to the appropriate areas, centering them on the mats.

**STEP 1**   Gently press a colored paper flower onto a white stamp pad.

**STEP 2**   Cut the flower into four equal quarters, and attach one to each corner of a photo.

**JEANETTE'S TIP**

Create your own B&T by stamping a fun design onto cardstock.

*For full Recipe see index pg. 127*

# Creative Team

## Layout Materials

12" × 12" Base Cardstock (2)
12" × 12" Cardstock (1)
12" × 12" B&T Paper (2)

## Left Page Dimensions

A  12" × 8"
B  5" × 12"
C  12" × 3"

## Right Page Dimensions

D  12" × 4"
E  5" × 12"
F  8" × 6"

## Photo Suggestions

1  5" × 7"
2  4" × 2¼" (5)
3  7" × 5"

## Suggested Title

1  11" × 2"

## Suggested Journaling

1  5" × 3"

**LEFT**

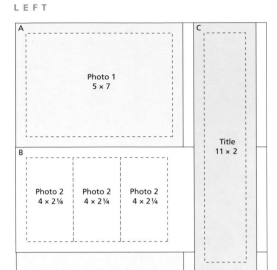

**RIGHT**

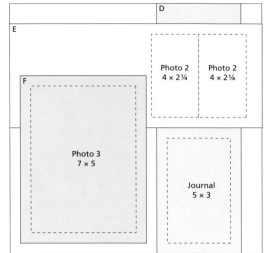

1  Using one 12" × 12" cardstock as your base, attach piece A to the left side of the page, keeping the edges flush.

2  Attach piece B, placing it 1" from the bottom of the page, keeping the side edges flush.

3  Attach piece C, placing it ½" from the right edge of the page, keeping the top and bottom edges flush.

4  Attach the specified photos (photos 1-2) to the appropriate areas.

1  Using one 12" × 12" cardstock as your base, attach piece D, placing it 1" from the right edge, keeping the top and bottom edges flush.

2  Attach piece E, placing it 1" from the top of the page, keeping the side edges flush.

3  Attach piece F to the bottom left corner of the page, placing it ½" from the bottom and left edges.

4  Attach the specified photos (photos 2-3) to the appropriate areas, centering them on the mats.

**JEANETTE'S TIP**

If you have fewer photos, add accents to fill the space.

**Letters in Relief.** *For full Recipe and Technique see index pg. 127*

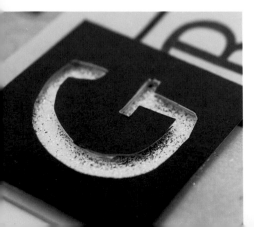

104

**G r o w i n g U P**

until June 2006

Coy and Cody

Since birth, Coy and Cody have been inseparable. Whenever one baby would start to cry either Matthew or I would pick him up and cuddle and feed him to try and get him to drift back into sleep. After time and time again we found out that neither baby would be able to fall back asleep until he was nestled next to his brother. Five years later when I dropped them off for their first day of Kindergarten I remember Coy insisting that his brother hold his hand as they walked through the intimidating giant double doors of their new school. Through teething, potty training, the terrible two's, playing in the park, and the first day of school, Coy and Cody have relied upon each other and I am sure that they will do so in their future endeavors together.

**BRING MANY PLEASING ELEMENTS TOGETHER FOR A CREATIVE TEAM EFFORT**

················· *Cutting Instructions* ·································································································

**B&T Paper**

| B 5 × 12 |
|---|
| E 5 × 12 |
| SCRAP |

**B&T Paper**

| A 12 × 8 | D 12 × 4 |
|---|---|

**Cardstock**

| C 12 × 3 | F 8 × 6 |
|---|---|
| | SCRAP |

ACCENTS AND PHOTOS PLAY ANY ROLE YOU LIKE WITH THIS STUNNING LAYOUT

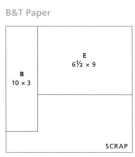

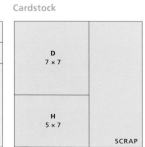

## Cutting Instructions

**B&T Paper**

| | |
|---|---|
| | **F**<br>6 × 8 |
| **A**<br>11½ × 4 | SCRAP |

**B&T Paper**

| | |
|---|---|
| | **E**<br>6½ × 9 |
| **B**<br>10 × 3 | SCRAP |

**Cardstock**

| |
|---|
| **C**<br>2 × 12 |
| **G**<br>2 × 12 |
| SCRAP |

**Cardstock**

| | |
|---|---|
| **D**<br>7 × 7 | |
| **H**<br>5 × 7 | SCRAP |

# Role Play

## Layout Materials

12" × 12" Base Cardstock (2)

12" × 12" Cardstock (2)

12" × 12" B&T Paper (2)

## Left Page Dimensions

A   11½" × 4"

B   10" × 3"

C   2" × 12"

D   7" × 7"

## Right Page Dimensions

E   6½" × 9"

F   6" × 8"

G   2" × 12"

H   5" × 7"

## Photo Suggestions

1   6" × 6"

2   3½" × 3½" (5)

3   4" × 6"

## Suggested Title

1   3" × 6"

## Suggested Journaling

1   4" × 3½"

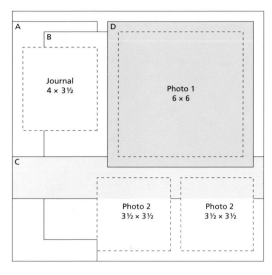

Layout diagram (LEFT): A, B, Journal 4 × 3½, D, Photo 1 6 × 6, C, Photo 2 3½ × 3½, Photo 2 3½ × 3½

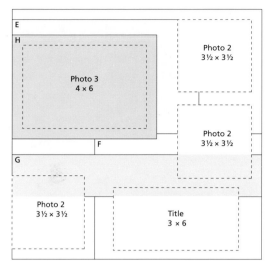

Layout diagram (RIGHT): E, H, Photo 3 4 × 6, Photo 2 3½ × 3½, Photo 2 3½ × 3½, F, G, Photo 2 3½ × 3½, Title 3 × 6

**1** Using one 12" × 12" cardstock as your base, attach piece A to the bottom left corner of the page, keeping the edges flush.

**2** Attach piece B, placing it 1" from the top and 1½" from the left edge of the page.

**3** Attach piece C, placing it 3" from the bottom of the page, keeping the side edges flush.

**4** Attach piece D, placing it ½" from the top and right edges of the page.

**5** Attach the specified photos (photos 1-2) to the appropriate areas, centering them on the mats.

**1** Using one 12" × 12" cardstock as your base, attach piece E to the left side of the page, placing it ½" from the top, keeping the left edges flush.

**2** Attach piece F to the bottom right corner of the page, keeping the edges flush.

**3** Attach piece G, placing it 3" from the bottom of the page, keeping the side edges flush. (If completing the two-page layout, be sure to line up the piece C and G strips across the pages.)

**4** Attach piece H to the left side of the page, placing it 1¼" from the top, keeping the left edges flush.

**5** Attach the specified photos (photos 2-3) to the appropriate areas, centering them on the mats.

## Beveled Photo Mat

**STEP 1** Align photo mat on the edge of a self-healing mat and press along the edge using an empressor tool. Repeat for all four sides.

**STEP 2** Swipe a coordinating stamp pad along the raised edges to highlight the empressed design.

*For full Recipe see index pg. 127*

# Grand Finale

## Layout Materials

12" × 12" Base Cardstock (2)
12" × 12" Cardstock (3)
12" × 12" B&T Paper (3)

## Left Page Dimensions

A 11" × 11½"
B 1" × 11½"
C 4½" × 11½"
D ½" × 11½"
E 3" × 3" (3)
F 2½" × 11½"

## Right Page Dimensions

G 11" × 8½"
H 1" × 7½"
I 4½" × 8½"
J ½" × 8½"
K 2½" × 8½"
L 7½" × 5½"
M 11" × 2½"
N ½" × 2½"
O 1" × 2½"

## Photo Suggestions

1 2½" × 2½" (3)
2 7" × 5"

## Suggested Title

1 2" × 11"

## Suggested Journaling

1 7½" × 2¼"

**JEANETTE'S TIP**

Hand journaling a border adds a personal touch to your page.

**Layering Cut-outs.** *For full Recipe and Technique see index pg. 127*

**LEFT**

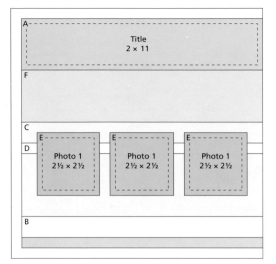

1 Using one 12" × 12" cardstock as your base, attach piece A, placing it ½" from the top of the page, keeping the right edges flush.

2 Attach piece B to piece A, placing it ½" from the bottom edge of piece A, keeping the right edges flush.

3 Attach piece C directly above piece B, keeping the right edges flush.

4 Attach piece D, placing it 1" from the top edge of piece C, keeping the right edges flush.

5 Attach the three pieces E, placing them 3" from the bottom of the page, 1¼" from the left edge of the page, and ½" from each other.

6 Attach piece F directly above piece C, keeping the edges flush.

7 Attach the specified photos (photos 1) to the appropriate areas, centering them on the mats.

**RIGHT**

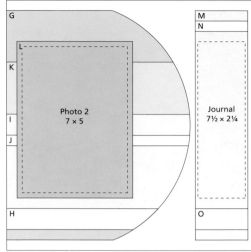

1 Attach piece H to piece G, placing it ½" from the bottom, keeping the left edges flush.

2 Attach piece I to piece G, placing it directly above piece H, keeping the left edges flush.

3 Attach piece J, placing it 1" from the top edge of piece I, keeping the left edges flush.

4 Attach piece K to piece G, placing it directly above piece I, keeping the left edges flush.

5 Using scissors, remove the excess from pieces H, I, J, and K by following the right contour of piece G.

6 Using one 12" × 12" cardstock as your base, attach piece G to the left side of the page, placing it ½" from the top of the page, keeping the left edges flush.

7 Attach piece L to the page, placing it 2" from the top and ½" from the left edge of the page.

8 Attach piece M, placing it ½" from the top, and ⅜" from the right edge of the page.

9 Attach piece N, placing it ½" from the top edge of piece M, keeping the side edges flush.

10 Attach piece O, placing it ½" from the bottom edge of piece M, keeping the side edges flush.

11 Attach the specified photo (photo 2) to the appropriate area, centering it on the mat.

*my beautiful*

# DAUGHTERS

*all the joy in my life comes from you*

sweet     smart     cute

A daughter is a precious
gift,
A blessing from above.
She's laughter,
warmth and feminine
charm.
She's thoughtfulness and
love.

A daughter brings a special
joy
That comes from deep
inside.
And as she grows to
womanhood
She fills your heart with
pride.

The love she gives so freely
Is a rare and beautiful gift.
She brings the sunshine
right indoors
And gives your heart a lift.

With every busy, happy year
She's dearer than before,
Through every
stage...through every age,
You love her more and more.

Breena & Sareena
September 2006

YOUR SUPPORTING CAST AND SHINING STARS TAKE A BIG BOW ACROSS THESE TWO PAGES.

---

*Cutting Instructions*

**B&T Paper**

D ½ × 11½
B 1 × 11½
H 1 × 7½
N ½ × 2½    O 1 × 2½   J ½ × 8½

SCRAP

**B&T Paper**

C 4½ × 11½

M 11 × 2½

I 4½ × 8½

SCRAP

**B&T Paper**

F 2½ × 11½

K 2½ × 8½

SCRAP

**Cardstock***

A 11 × 11½

SCRAP

**Cardstock***

5

G 11 × 8½

5

SCRAP

**Cardstock**

E 3 × 3   E 3 × 3   E 3 × 3

L 7½ × 5½

SCRAP

*Identical papers

FIRST swim meet

Makayla was so nervous for her first swim meet in Spanish Fork, but with Melody and Megan there cheering her on, those nerves slightly eased. We always knew that Makayla was a fast swimmer, we just didn't realize how fast she really is! She won three out of the four events that she participated in. She was even placed as anchor in an older age division in the Freestyle Relay. It was so fun to watch her prepare for a race. She would climb onto the platform, get into position, and if you listened close enough, you can hear her sing the World Cup chant to herself. Her times were so impressive that she was invited to compete in the Utah County Invitational Swim Meet, the youngest swimmer from Spanish Fork to be invited! Who knows, our little Mak-Attack may be the next Michael Phelps!

- 2nd- 25m Freestyle
- 1st- 25m Breast Stroke
- 1st- 25m Back Stroke
- 1st- Freestyle Relay (anchor)

## Cutting Instructions

**B&T Paper**

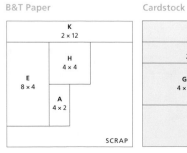

| | |
|---|---|
| D 8 × 2 | B 4 × 10 |
| | I 4 × 8 |
| F 4 × 4 | SCRAP |

**B&T Paper**

| | |
|---|---|
| | K 2 × 12 |
| E 8 × 4 | H 4 × 4 |
| | A 4 × 2 |
| | SCRAP |

**Cardstock**

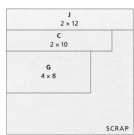

| |
|---|
| J 2 × 12 |
| C 2 × 10 |
| G 4 × 8 |
| SCRAP |

# Understood

## Layout Materials

12" × 12" Base
Cardstock (2)

12" × 12"
Cardstock (1)

12" × 12" B&T
Paper (2)

## Left Page Dimensions

A  4" × 2"
B  4" × 10"
C  2" × 10"
D  8" × 2"
E  8" × 4"

## Right Page Dimensions

F  4" × 4"
G  4" × 8"
H  4" × 4"
I  4" × 8"
J  2" × 12"
K  2" × 12"

## Photo Suggestions

1  3½" × 5" (2)
2  8" × 6"
3  3" × 3" (2)
4  5" × 3½" (2)

## Suggested Title

1  1½" × 9½"

## Suggested Journaling

1  3½" × 7½"

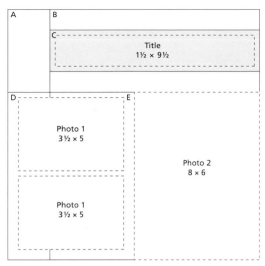

Title
1½ × 9½

Photo 1
3½ × 5

Photo 1
3½ × 5

Photo 2
8 × 6

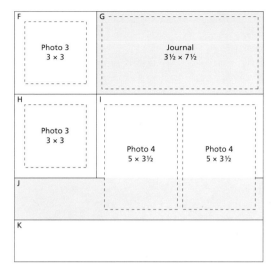

Photo 3
3 × 3

Journal
3½ × 7½

Photo 3
3 × 3

Photo 4
5 × 3½

Photo 4
5 × 3½

**1** Using one 12" × 12" cardstock as your base, attach piece A to the top left corner of the page, keeping the edges flush.

**2** Attach piece B to the top right corner of the page, keeping the edges flush.

**3** Attach piece C to the center of piece B, placing it 1" from the top, keeping the right edges flush.

**4** Attach piece D to the bottom left corner of the page, keeping the edges flush.

**5** Attach piece E directly to the right of piece D, keeping the bottom edges flush.

**6** Attach the specified photos (photos 1-2) to the appropriate areas.

**1** Using one 12" × 12" cardstock as your base, attach piece F to the top left corner of the page, keeping the edges flush.

**2** Attach piece G to the top right corner of the page, keeping the edges flush.

**3** Attach piece H to the left side of the page directly below piece F, keeping the edges flush.

**4** Attach piece I directly below piece G, keeping the right edges flush.

**5** Attach piece J directly below pieces H and I, keeping the side edges flush.

**6** Attach piece K to the bottom of the page, keeping the edges flush.

**7** Attach the specified photos (photos 3-4) to the appropriate areas, centering them on the mats.

## Water Effect with Detail Embossing Powder

**STEP 1** Sponge a watermark ink over the image in your photo.

**STEP 2** Pour clear Detail Embossing Powder over inked area and heat with heat gun until the powder melts.

JEANETTE'S TIP

Build a fun title by placing some of your words vertically and some horizontally.

*For full Recipe see index pg. 128*

# Swing Rhythm

## Layout Materials

12" × 12" Base Cardstock (2)
12" × 12" Cardstock (2)
12" × 12" B&T Paper (2)

### Left Page Dimensions

A  5" × 12"
B  1½" × 12"
C  5½" × 12"
D  ½" × 12" (2)
E  2½" × 3"
F  6½" × 4½"

### Right Page Dimensions

G  3" × 12"
H  ½" × 12"
I  6½" × 4½" (2)
J  4" × 12"
K  1½" × 12"
L  2½" × 3½"
M  ½" × 3½"
N  2" × 2½"

## Photo Suggestions

1  6" × 4" (3)
2  3½" × 2½" (4)

## Suggested Title

1  2" × 6"

## Suggested Journaling

1  2" × 2½"
2  1½" × 2"

### JEANETTE'S TIP

Make your title stand out by mounting each letter on its own mat.

**Stamp Shading.** *For full Recipe and Technique see index pg. 128*

## LEFT

A

D | Title 2 × 6 | E | Journal 2 × 2½

B | F

C

Photo 1 6 × 4

Photo 2 3½ × 2½ | Photo 2 3½ × 2½

D

1  Using one 12" × 12" cardstock as your base, attach piece A to the top of the page, keeping the edges flush.

2  Attach piece B directly below piece A, keeping the edges flush.

3  Attach piece C to the bottom of the page, keeping the edges flush.

4  Attach one piece D to piece A, placing it 2½" from the top of the page, keeping the side edges flush.

5  Attach remaining piece D to piece C, placing it 1½" from the bottom of the page, keeping the side edges flush.

6  Attach piece E to upper piece D, placing it 1½" from the top and right edges of the page.

7  Attach piece F, placing it ½" from the bottom and 1" from the left edge of the page.

8  Attach the specified photos (photos 1-2) to the appropriate areas, centering them on the mats.

## RIGHT

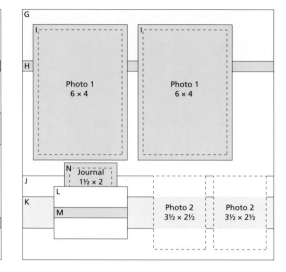

G

I | I

H

Photo 1 6 × 4 | Photo 1 6 × 4

N | Journal 1½ × 2

J

L

K

M | Photo 2 3½ × 2½ | Photo 2 3½ × 2½

1  Using one 12" × 12" cardstock as your base, attach piece G to the top of the page, keeping the edges flush.

2  Attach piece H to the bottom of piece G, keeping the side edges flush.

3  Attach both piece I mats to the page, placing them ¾" from the top, ½" from the left edge and ½" from each other.

4  Attach piece J to the bottom of the page, keeping the edges flush.

5  Attach piece K to the center of piece J, keeping the side edges flush.

6  Attach piece L to piece K, placing it 1½" from the left and 1" from the bottom of the page, adhering only on the side and bottom edges to form a pocket.

7  Attach piece M to the center of piece L, keeping the side edges flush.

8  Insert piece N into the pocket formed by pieces L and M.

9  Attach the specified photos (photos 1-2) to the appropriate areas, centering them on the mats.

STAGGERED ELEMENTS BRING A RHYTHMIC PRESENTATION TO EACH PAGE

Text visible in layout:

FALL

We really enjoy the outdoors. Each year when the leaves begin to change color we try and take a weekend trip to the mountains. This particular trip was to Keystone, Colorado. It was absolutely gorgeous.

the andersons

September 27, 2005

---

...... Cutting Instructions ......

**B&T Paper**

| A<br>5 × 12 |
| J<br>4 × 12 |
| SCRAP |

**B&T Paper**

| C<br>5½ × 12 |
| G<br>3 × 12 |
| L<br>2½ × 3½ |
| SCRAP |

**Cardstock**

| B 1½ × 12 |
| K 1½ × 12 |
| SCRAP |

**Cardstock**

| D ½ × 12 | | E<br>2½ × 3 |
| F<br>6½ × 4½ | | |
| | | N<br>2 × 2½ |
| H ½ × 12 | | |
| I<br>6½ × 4½ | I<br>6½ × 4½ | |
| M ½ × 3½ | | SCRAP |

The Morenson's

Growing up, my mom would always
get my sisters and me coordinating
Easter Outfits.
She would even go as far as getting gloves,
bonnets and purses.
I loved this tradition so much that I decided
to carry it on in my family, minus the bonnets!
I was so thrilled on Easter Morning to see
how happy and how beautiful my family
looked. I was even able to take several
pictures without hearing one complaint!
Although, I think that Kyle bribed
the kids to be good!

Kimberly Claire

Libby

Conner James

EASTER

SUNDAY
2006

**PHOTOS OF THE SAME SIZE DOUBLE FOR A PLEASING SHADOW EFFECT**

## Cutting Instructions

**B&T Paper**

F
2 × 5

J
2 × 4½

A
12 × 1

SCRAP

**B&T Paper**

G
1¾ × 1¾

B
12 × 1½

H
12 × 1½

SCRAP

**B&T Paper**

D
3 × 12

K
3 × 4½

L
8 × 7½

SCRAP

**Cardstock***

E
1 × 12

M
1 × 12

I
12 × 4½

SCRAP

**Cardstock***

C
10¾ × 8

SCRAP

*Identical papers

# Shadow

**Flower Tag with Liquid Glass**

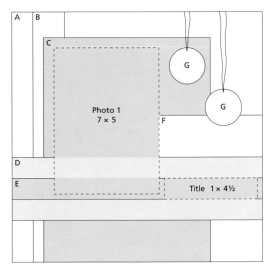

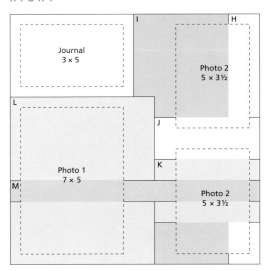

## Layout Materials

12" × 12" Base
Cardstock (2)

12" × 12"
Cardstock (2)

12" × 12" B&T
Paper (3)

## Left Page Dimensions

A  12" × 1"
B  12" × 1½"
C  10¾" × 8"
D  3" × 12"
E  1" × 12"
F  2" × 5"
G  1¾" circle (2)

## Right Page Dimensions

H  12" × 1½"
I  12" × 4½"
J  2" × 4½"
K  3" × 4½"
L  8" × 7½"
M  1" × 12"

## Photo Suggestions

1  7" × 5" (2)
2  5" × 3½" (2)

## Suggested Title

1  1" × 4½"

## Suggested Journaling

1  3" × 5"

### Left diagram labels

A B
C
G
G
Photo 1
7 × 5
F
D
E
Title  1 × 4½

### Right diagram labels

I H
Journal
3 × 5
Photo 2
5 × 3½
L
Photo 1
7 × 5
J
K
M
Photo 2
5 × 3½

### Left instructions

1  Using one 12" × 12" cardstock as your base, attach piece A to the left side of the page, keeping the edges flush.

2  Attach piece B directly to the right of piece A, keeping the top and bottom edges flush.

3  Attach piece C, placing it 1½" from the left edge, keeping the bottom edges flush.

4  Attach piece D, placing it 2" from the bottom of the page, keeping the side edges flush.

5  Attach piece E to the center of piece D, keeping the side edges flush.

6  Attach piece F to the right side of the page, directly above piece D, keeping the right edges flush.

7  Attach fiber to pieces G placing them on the upper right corner of the page as illustrated if desired.

8  Attach the specified photo (photo 1) to the appropriate area.

### Right instructions

1  Using one 12" × 12" cardstock as your base, attach piece H to the right side of the page, keeping the edges flush.

2  Attach piece I directly to the left of piece H, keeping the top and bottom edges flush.

3  Attach piece J to the right side of the page, placing it 5" from the top, keeping the right edges flush.

4  Attach piece K to the right side of the page directly below piece J, keeping the right edges flush.

5  Attach piece L to the bottom left corner of the page, keeping the edges flush.

6  Attach piece M to pieces K and L, placing it 3" from the bottom edge, keeping the side edges flush. (If completing the two-page layout, be sure to line up the piece E and M strips across the pages.)

7  Attach the specified photos (photos 1-2) to the appropriate areas.

**STEP 1**  Attach a paper flower to a metal-rimmed tag using an oversized brad for the center.

**STEP 2**  Holding the petals out of the way, flood the tag and flower with Liquid Glass. Allow the petals to gently sink into the Liquid Glass. Let dry.

### JEANETTE'S TIP

Circle elements on the layout are often embellishment placeholders. Cut them from matching or contrasting paper and decorate!

*For full Recipe see index pg. 128*

# Overture

## Layout Materials

12" × 12" Base Cardstock (2)
12" × 12" Cardstock (3)
12" × 12" B&T Paper (2)

## Left Page Dimensions

A  8" × 8"
B  7½" × 7½"
C  7" × 7"
D  4½" × 8"
    (4" × 8" torn)
E  2½" × 8"
F  1" × 8"

## Right Page Dimensions

G  8" × 5"
H  6½" × 4½"
I  8" × 3"
J  4½" × 12" (4" × 12" torn)
K  2½" × 12"
L  1" × 12"

## Photo Suggestions

1  6" × 6"
2  3" × 3" (4)
3  6" × 4"
4  2" × 2" (3)

## Suggested Title

1  1" × 6"

## Suggested Journaling

1  3" × 3"

**LEFT**

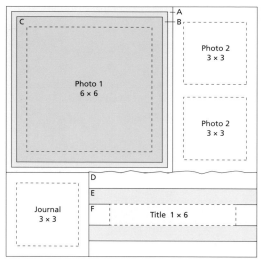

1  Decoratively tear or cut no more than ½" from piece D as shown in the cutting diagrams.

2  Using one 12" × 12" cardstock as your base, attach piece A to the top left corner of the page, keeping the edges flush.

3  Attach piece B to the center of piece A.

4  Attach piece C to the center of piece B.

5  Attach piece D to the bottom right corner of the page, keeping the edges flush.

6  Attach piece E across the center of piece D, keeping the right edges flush.

7  Attach piece F across the center of piece E, keeping the right edges flush.

8  Attach the specified photos (photos 1-2) to the appropriate areas, centering them on the mats.

**RIGHT**

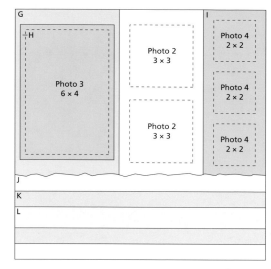

1  Decoratively tear or cut no more than ½" from piece J as shown in the cutting diagrams.

2  Using one 12" × 12" cardstock as your base, attach piece G to the top left corner of the page, keeping the edges flush.

3  Attach piece H to piece G, placing it ¾" from the top, centered side-to-side.

4  Attach piece I to the top right corner of the page, keeping the edges flush.

5  Attach piece J across the bottom of the page, keeping the edges flush.

6  Attach piece K across the center of piece J, keeping the side edges flush. (If completing the two-page layout, be sure to line up the piece E and K strips across the pages.)

7  Attach piece L across the center of piece K, keeping the side edges flush. (If completing the two-page layout, be sure to line up the piece F and L strips across the pages.)

8  Attach the specified photos (photos 2-4) to the appropriate areas, centering them on the mats.

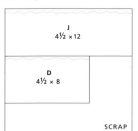

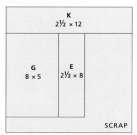

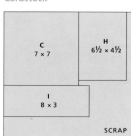

Blake is my sweet little baby. With his big blue eyes and head full of dark hair could he be any more adorable. He is such a happy baby, always smiling and giggling. The expressions on his face make me laugh. I sure love this tiny guy. My little one.

My *Little* ONE

BLAKE

**FILL UP THE PAGES WITH A SURPRISINGLY SIMPLE ARRAY OF PIECES**

.................... *Cutting Instructions* ........................................................................

**B&T Paper**

J
4½ × 12

D
4½ × 8

SCRAP

**B&T Paper**

L 1 × 12

A
8 × 8

F 1 × 8

SCRAP

**Cardstock***

K
2½ × 12

G
8 × 5

E
2½ × 8

SCRAP

**Cardstock***

B
7½ × 7½

SCRAP

**Cardstock**

C
7 × 7

H
6½ × 4½

I
8 × 3

SCRAP

*Identical papers*

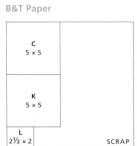
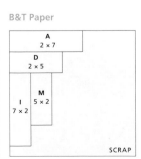

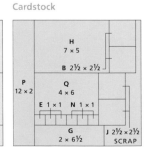

## Cutting Instructions

**B&T Paper**

| | |
|---|---|
| C 5 × 5 | |
| K 5 × 5 | |
| L 2½ × 2 | SCRAP |

**B&T Paper**

| | |
|---|---|
| A 2 × 7 | |
| D 2 × 5 | |
| I 7 × 2 | M 5 × 2 |
| | SCRAP |

**Cardstock**

| |
|---|
| F 5 × 12 |
| O 12 × 5 |
| SCRAP |

**Cardstock**

| | |
|---|---|
| H 7 × 5 | |
| | B 2½ × 2½ |
| P 12 × 2 | Q 4 × 6 |
| E 1 × 1   N 1 × 1 | |
| G 2 × 6½ | J 2½ × 2½  SCRAP |

118

# Salsa

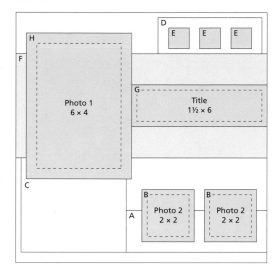

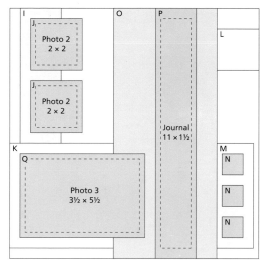

**Layering with Re-inker**

**STEP 1** Stamp image on cardstock. Pour re-inker on a sponge and dab onto stamp.

**STEP 2** Stamp image on a transparency. Because of the re-inker the stamp will be extra moist so use caution when stamping to avoid slippage. Allow to dry. Layer the transparency and cardstock, lining up the images.

## Left Page

*Layout Materials*

12" × 12" Base Cardstock (2)

12" × 12" Cardstock (2)

12" × 12" B&T Paper (2)

*Left Page Dimensions*

A  2" × 7"
B  2½" × 2½" (2)
C  5" × 5"
D  2" × 5"
E  1" × 1" (3)
F  5" × 12"
G  2" × 6"
H  7" × 5"

*Right Page Dimensions*

I  7" × 2"
J  2½" × 2½" (2)
K  5" × 5"
L  2" × 2½"
M  5" × 2"
N  1" × 1" (3)
O  12" × 5"
P  12" × 2"
Q  4" × 6"

*Photo Suggestions*

1  6" × 4"
2  2" × 2" (4)
3  3½" × 5½"

*Suggested Title*

1  1½" × 6"

*Suggested Journaling*

1  11" × 1½"

### Left instructions

1  Using one 12" × 12" cardstock as your base, attach piece A to the page, placing it ½" from the bottom, keeping the right edges flush.

2  Attach the two pieces B to the page, placing them ½" from the bottom and right edges of piece A and ½" from each other.

3  Attach piece C to the page, placing it ½" from the bottom and ¼" from the left edge.

4  Attach piece D to the page, placing it ¼" from the top and right edges.

5  Attach three pieces E to piece D, placing them ½" from the side edges, ½" from the top, and ½" from each other.

6  Attach piece F across the page, placing it 2" from the top of the page, keeping the side edges flush.

7  Attach piece G to the center of piece F keeping the right edges flush.

8  Attach piece H to the page, placing it 1" from the top and ½" from the left edge.

9  Attach the specified photos (photos 1-2) to the appropriate areas, centering them on the mats.

### Right instructions

1  Using one 12" × 12" cardstock as your base, attach piece I to the page, placing it ½" from the left edge, keeping the top edges flush.

2  Attach two pieces J to the page, placing them ½" from the top, 1" from the left edge, and ½" from each other.

3  Attach piece K to the page, placing it ½" from the bottom of the page, keeping the left edges flush.

4  Attach piece L to the page, placing it 1" from the top of the page, keeping the right edges flush.

5  Attach piece M to the page, placing it ½" from the bottom and ¼" from the right edge.

6  Attach the three pieces N to piece M, placing them ½" from the top and bottom edges, ½" from the right and ½" from each other.

7  Attach piece O to the page, placing it 2" from the right side of the page, keeping the top and bottom edges flush.

8  Attach piece P to the page, placing it 3" from the right side of the page, keeping the top and bottom edges flush.

9  Attach piece Q to the page, placing it ½" from the left edge and 1" from the bottom.

10  Attach the appropriate photos (photos 2-3) to the appropriate areas, centering them on the mats.

---

**JEANETTE'S TIP**

Add variation to your page by curling and inking the edges of your paper.

*For full Recipe see index pg. 128*

# Techniques and Recipes

Want more ideas and inspiration? Visit Jeanette online for author insights, all-new artwork, and much more! **jeanettelynton.com**

## LEADING LADY (page 16)

*Technique: Jazzed Up Embellishments*

Use precut library pockets to accent your photos. Mat the photo on the pocket, and then fold the extra paper behind the photo forming a flap. Add a photo clip, held on by a brad, to keep the flap closed. Beneath the flap add journaling or extra photos of your event.

*Recipe*

My Acrylix® Stamp Set, Rustic Alphabet
Just Chillin' Paper Packet
Just Chillin' My Stickease™ Assortment
Chocolate Cardstock
Chocolate Exclusive Inks™ Pad
Desert Sand Exclusive Inks™ Pad
Dimensional Elements Ribbon Accents
Fancy Cuts™ File Folders
Designer Ribbon Rounds™ Cocoa Collection
Silver My Accents™ Accessory Kit
Colonial White Waxy Flax
Paper Circle Tags
Bigger Brads Basic Collection
Silver Brads
Silver Eyelets
Liquid Glass
White Hemp
3-D Foam Squares
Photo Clips
Thread

## SIDELINE SURPRISE (page 18)

*Recipe*

My Acrylix® Stamp Set, Best Friends
My Acrylix® Stamp Set, Wedding
White Daisy Textured Cardstock
Bamboo Cardstock
Bamboo Exclusive Inks™ Pad
Buttercup Exclusive Inks™ Pad
Heavenly Blue Exclusive Inks™ Pad
Mulberry Paper
Just Blooms™ Autumn Daisy Paper Flowers
Buttercup My Accents™ Accessory Kit
Vanilla Cream Waxy Flax
Buttercup Eyelets
Heavenly Blue Eyelets
Rubber Brayer
Piercing Tool

## IN THE GROOVE (page 20)

*Technique: Stamping on Twill Ribbon*

Choose image or phrase to stamp. Generously ink your stamp and carefully stamp images onto the twill, pressing firmly and slowly to allow the ink to absorb into the ribbon before lifting stamp. Test the ribbon before stamping on your final project to ensure the ink does not bleed.

*Recipe*

My Acrylix® Stamp Set, Calendar
My Acrylix® Stamp Set, Vroom Caps
My Acrylix® Stamp Set, Solos™ "T"
My Acrylix® Stamp Set, Solos™ "J"
My Acrylix® Stamp Set, Solos™ "C"
My Acrylix® Stamp Set, Sans Small Caps
My Acrylix® Stamp Set, Sans Small Lowercase
My Acrylix® Stamp Set, Classic Caps
Pawsitively Pals Paper Packet
Grey Wool Cardstock
Desert Sand Exclusive Inks™ Pad
Grey Wool Exclusive Inks™ Pad
Colonial White My Accents™ Accessory Kit
Ribbon Rounds™ White Daisy Collection
Natural Hemp
Photo Clips
Photo Hangers
Round Sponge
Thread

## PROOF PREVIEW (page 22)

*Recipe*

Snips & Snails Paper Packet
Snips & Snails My Stickease™ Assortment
Cocoa Cardstock
Chocolate Exclusive Inks™ Pad
Dimensional Elements Basic Shapes
Dimensional Elements Slide Frames
Ribbon Rounds™ White Daisy Collection
Colonial White My Accents™ Accessory Kit
Pewter My Accents™ Accessory Kit
Bigger Brads Basic Collection
3-D Foam Squares
Pewter Eyelets
Photo Clips
Hinges
Zippers
Thread

## SYMPHONY SWEET (page 24)

*Technique: Tone-on-Tone Stamping*

Stamp fun little journaling sentiments in tone-on-tone colors to add subtle wording details without distracting from your photos. To achieve this look use a stamp pad ink that matches your cardstock.

*Recipe*

My Acrylix® Stamp Set, Solos™ "B"
My Acrylix® Stamp Set, Kid Power
Abundance Paper Packet
Goldrush Cardstock
Cocoa Exclusive Inks™ Pad
Autumn Terracotta My Accents™ Accessory Kit
Designer Ribbon Rounds™ Cocoa Collection
Thread

## PERFECT PRELUDE (page 26)

*Recipe*

My Acrylix® Stamp Set, Seasonal Thoughts
My Acrylix® Stamp Set, Spring
Best Friends Forever Paper Packet
White Daisy Textured Cardstock
Blush Exclusive Inks™ Pad
Hollyhock Exclusive Inks™ Pad
Dimensional Elements Ribbon Accents
White Daisy My Accents™ Accessory Kit
Bigger Brads Basic Collection
White Daisy Eyelets
⅜" White Daisy Organdy Ribbon
Thread
White Paint

## POWERFUL TRIO (page 28)

*Technique: Coloring Linen*

To create a customized color of linen, add a chosen color of ink liberally and apply evenly with a round sponge or brayer until the desired color is achieved.

*Recipe*

Sweet Harmony Paper Packet
Sweet Harmony My Stickease™ Assortment
Sweet Leaf Textured Cardstock
Spring Iris Cardstock
Colonial White Exclusive Inks™ Pad
Sweet Leaf Exclusive Inks™ Pad
StickStock™ Linen
Dimensional Elements Classic Alphabet
White Daisy My Accents™ Accessory Kit
Colonial White Waxy Flax
White Paint

## TIMELINE (page 30)

*Recipe*

My Acrylix® Stamp Set, Welcome to the Neighborhood
My Acrylix® Stamp Set, Solos™ "L"
My Acrylix® Stamp Set, Solos™ "O"
My Acrylix® Stamp Set, Solos™ "V"
My Acrylix® Stamp Set, Solos™ "E"
Baby Pink Background and Texture Paper
Blush Textured Cardstock
Bamboo Cardstock
Chocolate Exclusive Inks™ Pad
Fancy Cuts™ Library Pockets
Just Blooms™ White Daisy Variety Pack
White Daisy My Accents™ Accessory Kit
Designer Ribbon Rounds™ Cocoa Collection
Organdy Ribbon Rounds™ Spring Harmony Collection
Organdy Ribbon Rounds™ Winter Classic Collection
Natural Hemp
3-D Foam Squares
Hinges
¼" Long Reach Punch
Round Sponge
White Acrylic Paint
Thread
Batting

## INTRODUCTION (page 32)

*Technique: Fraying Twill*

Fray the edges of twill, adhesive-backed fabric, by carefully pulling off some fibers on the edges with a piercing tool. Add a distressed look to the twill by adding some additional color with a Sponge Dauber and light-colored ink. To print journaling from your computer onto the twill adhesive-backed fabric, adhere tape around the edge that enters the printer first, and be sure to use the heavyweight paper setting.

*Recipe*

My Acrylix® Stamp Set, Happy Harvest
Abundance Paper Packet
Abundance My Stickease™ Assortment
New England Ivy Cardstock
Autumn Terracotta Cardstock
Autumn Terracotta Exclusive Inks™ Pad
New England Ivy Exclusive Inks™ Pad
StickStock™ Twill
New England Ivy Waxy Flax
Autumn Terracotta Eyelets
Dimensional Elements Bookplates
Dimensional Elements Basic Shapes

## MEDLEY (page 34)

*Recipe*

My Acrylix® Stamp Set, Rustic Alphabet
My Acrylix® Stamp Set, Sketchy Numbers
Amethyst Cardstock
Buttercup Cardstock
Hydrangea Cardstock
White Daisy Cardstock
Background and Texture Summer Carnival Combo Pack
Amethyst Exclusive Inks™ Pad
Hydrangea Exclusive Inks™ Pad
Hydrangea Exclusive Inks™ Marker
Amethyst Waxy Flax
Paper Circle Tags
Sponge Daubers

## SERENADE (page 36)

*Technique: 12" × 12" File Folders*

Use a 12" × 12" file folder to hold extra photos or memorabilia that will not fit on your scrapbook page but may not warrant a page of their own. Create a layout on the outside of the folder and add even more pictures and memories to the inside in the form of a collage or additional layout.

*Recipe*

My Acrylix® Stamp Set, Festive Thoughts
Hollydays Paper Packet
White Daisy Textured Cardstock
Bamboo Cardstock
Black Cardstock
White Daisy Cardstock
Chocolate Exclusive Inks™ Pad
Black Exclusive Inks™ Pad
Dimensional Elements Basic Shapes
Season's Greetings Ribbon Rounds™
Pewter My Accents™ Accessory Kit
Black My Accents™ Accessory Kit
Sassy Strands™ White Daisy Collection
Pewter Eyelets
Hinges

## JAZZY COMBINATION (page 38)

*Recipe*

My Acrylix® Stamp Set, Outdoor Trek
My Acrylix® Stamp Set, Beauty Seen
My Acrylix® Stamp Set, Classic Caps
My Reflections Collection™ Graduation Kit
Building Blocks Paper Packet
Outdoor Denim Cardstock
Spring Iris Cardstock
White Daisy Cardstock
Black Cardstock
True Black Archival Exclusive Inks™ Pad
Outdoor Denim Exclusive Inks™ Pad
Spring Iris Exclusive Inks™ Pad
Pewter My Accents™ Accessory Kit
Watercolor Pencils
Large Waterbrush

## ENSEMBLE PIECE (page 40)

*Technique: Coloring Black and White Photos*

Print the photo in black and white or sepia tones on matte-finished paper. Color the specified area by chalking using a sponge applicator and gently adding color highlights to the photo.

*Recipe*

White Daisy Cardstock
Cocoa Cardstock
Chocolate Cardstock
Brown Bag Cardstock
Bamboo Cardstock
Desert Sand Cardstock
Chocolate Exclusive Inks™ Pad
Cocoa Exclusive Inks™ Pad
Black Exclusive Inks™ Pad
My Legacy Writer® Black Pen Set
Dimensional Elements Classic Alphabet
Dimensional Elements Ribbon Accents
Designer Ribbon Rounds™ Cocoa Collection
Spring Soft Chalks
Liquid Glass
Paper Circle Tags
Pewter Eyelets
Straight Pin
Thread

## CONCERTO (page 42)

*Recipe*

My Acrylix® Stamp Set, Spirit of '76
My Acrylix® Stamp Set, Calendar
Independence Paper Packet
Barn Red Cardstock
Cocoa Exclusive Inks™ Pad
Outdoor Denim Exclusive Inks™ Pad
Barn Red Exclusive Inks™ Pad
Clear Embossing Powder
Pewter My Accents™ Accessory Kit
Organdy Ribbon Rounds™ Autumn Harvest Collection
Dimensional Elements Basic Shapes
Dimensional Elements Bookplates
Sponge Daubers

## THREE-PART HARMONY (page 44)

*Technique: Make Your Own Buckle*

Create the look of a belt buckle with two photo hangers. Thread a ribbon through two photo hangers and around the page, and secure to the back side. Anchor the outer photo hanger with a brad, piercing the ribbon first with a piercing tool.

*Recipe*

My Acrylix® Stamp Set, Calendar
My Acrylix® Stamp Set, Private Eye Tiny Lowercase
My Acrylix® Stamp Set, Sans Small Caps
Textured Cardstock Autumn Harvest Combo Pack
Background and Texture Autumn Harvest Combo Pack
White Daisy Cardstock
Autumn Terracotta Exclusive Inks™ Pad
Dimensional Elements Bookplates
Dimensional Elements Basic Shapes
Just Blooms™ Autumn Daisy Paper Flowers
White Daisy Grosgrain Ribbon
Autumn Terracotta My Accents™ Accessory Kit
Photo Hangers
Photo Clips
Thread

## MINUET (page 46)

*Recipe*

My Acrylix® Stamp Set, Sports
Background and Texture Spring Harmony Combo Pack
Crystal Blue Cardstock
Olive Cardstock
Chocolate Cardstock
Bamboo Cardstock
White Daisy Cardstock
Chocolate Exclusive Inks™ Pad
Olive Exclusive Inks™ Pad
Crystal Blue Exclusive Inks™ Pad
Bamboo Exclusive Inks™ Pad
Chocolate Exclusive Inks™ Marker
Olive Exclusive Inks™ Marker
Dimensional Elements Classic Alphabet
Dimensional Elements Bookplates
Dimensional Elements Basic Shapes
Dimensional Elements Slide Frames
White Daisy Grosgrain Ribbon
Pewter Eyelets
Photo Clips
Hinges
Sandpaper

## DYNAMIC DUO (page 48)

*Technique: Creating Fun Photo Mats*

Use the Coluzzle® File Folder Template to create fun and interesting photo mats. Cut your mat an extra ½" bigger on the side you desire to place your tab. Place the Coluzzle® Cutting Mat under your project. Place your template over your photo mat positioned where you would like to create the tab. Use the Coluzzle® Swivel Knife in the precut groove to trim the piece to the specified shape.

*Recipe*

My Acrylix® Stamp Set, Season Of Color
My Acrylix® Stamp Set, Sketchy Caps
My Acrylix® Stamp Set, Sketchy Lowercase
Textured Cardstock Autumn Harvest Combo Pack
Bamboo Cardstock
White Daisy Cardstock
Background and Texture Winter Classic Combo Pack
Cranberry Exclusive Inks™ Pad
Bamboo Exclusive Inks™ Pad
Outdoor Denim Exclusive Inks™ Pad
Tinted Embossing Pad
Clear Embossing Powder
Silver Embossing Powder
Pewter My Accents™ Accessory Kit
Small Embossing Stylus
Hinges
Coluzzle® File Folder

## MONOLOGUE (page 52)

*Recipe*

My Acrylix® Stamp Set, Vroom Caps
My Acrylix® Stamp Set, Rustic Alphabet
My Acrylix® Stamp Set, Sans Small Lowercase
My Acrylix® Stamp Set, Sans Small Caps
Pawsitively Pals Paper Packet
Background and Texture Summer Celebration Combo Pack
White Daisy Textured Cardstock
Cocoa Cardstock
Vellum
Dimensional Elements Basic Shapes
Dimensional Elements Ribbon Accents
Designer Ribbon Rounds™ Cocoa Collection
Pewter My Accents™ Accessory Kit
Liquid Glass
Natural Hemp
Hinges
Photo Clips
Photo Hangers
Thread

## EVERYTHING IN ITS PLACE (page 54)

*Technique: Painting Photo Clips*

Take any photo clip or metal accent and make it coordinate with the layout by painting with an acrylic paint or spray paint.

*Recipe*

My Acrylix® Stamp Set, Precious Alphabet
My Acrylix® Stamp Set, Solos "B"
My Acrylix® Stamp Set, Sans Small Lowercase
My Acrylix® Stamp Set, Sans Small Caps
Hollyhock Cardstock
Blush Cardstock
Cocoa Cardstock
Bamboo Cardstock
Cocoa Exclusive Inks™ Pad
Bamboo Exclusive Inks™ Pad
Blush Exclusive Inks™ Pad
Hollyhock Exclusive Inks™ Pad
Dimensional Elements Ribbon Accents
Fancy Cuts™ File Folders
Ribbon Rounds™ White Daisy Collection
Desert Sand Eyelets
Photo Clips
Paint
String

## CONCLUSION COMBO (page 56)

*Recipe*

My Acrylix® Stamp Set, Sans Small Caps
My Acrylix® Stamp Set, Sans Small Lowercase
My Acrylix® Stamp Set, Best Friends
My Acrylix® Stamp Set, Snapshot
My Acrylix® Stamp Set, Heritage
Discovery Paper Packet
Discovery My Stickease™ Assortment
StazOn® Ink Pad
White Daisy My Accents™ Accessory Kit
Colonial White Waxy Flax
Watermelon Waxy Flax
Dimensional Elements Bookplates
Round Sponge
White Paint
Thread

## DIALOGUE (page 58)

*Technique: Stippling*

Add gradient depth to accents or papers with a stipple brush. Using a darker ink color than the base color, stipple each letter in a straight up-and-down motion, stippling more at the bottom and less as you go upward. Keep adding ink until the desired color is achieved.

*Recipe*

Rustic Trail Paper Packet
Autumn Terracotta Cardstock
Cocoa Exclusive Inks™ Pad
My Legacy Writer® Black Pen Set
Pewter My Accents™ Accessory Kit
Dimensional Elements Classic Alphabet
Natural Hemp
Photo Clips

## FIESTA (PAGE 60)

*Recipe*

My Acrylix® Stamp Set, Playful Lowercase
My Acrylix® Stamp Set, Solos™ "D"
Denim Days My Stickease™
Background and Texture Winter Classic Combo Pack
Background and Texture Summer Celebration Combo Pack
Sunny Yellow Cardstock
Colonial White Cardstock
White Daisy Cardstock
Black Cardstock
Sunny Yellow Exclusive Inks™ Pad
Black Exclusive Inks™ Pad
Cranberry Exclusive Inks™ Pad
Black My Accents™ Accessory Kit
Cranberry My Accents™ Accessory Kit
Colonial White Waxy Flax
Just Blooms™ White Daisy Variety Pack
Black Gingham Ribbon
Window Charms™
3-D Foam Squares
Photo Hangers

## FANTASTIC FIVE (page 62)

*Technique: Sponge Daubing*

To add a subtle highlight effect to your accents, sponge the edges of each piece using Sponge Daubers and inks. Experiment with a scrap piece of paper to achieve the desired look. Ink color that is similar to your paper will give a shaded effect; different ink colors will add contrast to your layout.

*Recipe*

My Acrylix® Stamp Set, Sans Small Caps
My Acrylix® Stamp Set, Sweet Flowers
Floral Tapestry Paper Packet
Bamboo Exclusive Inks™ Pad
Orchid Exclusive Inks™ Pad
Twilight Exclusive Inks™ Pad
Garden Green Exclusive Inks™ Pad
Holiday Red Exclusive Inks™ Pad
Creative Clips™
Dimensional Elements Classic Alphabet
Dimensional Elements Simple Alphabet
Dimensional Elements Bookplates
Dimensional Elements Ribbon Accents
Colonial White My Accents™ Accessory Kit
Garden Green My Accents™ Accessory Kit
Olive Waxy Flax
3-D Foam Squares

## UP THE TEMPO (page 64)

*Recipe*

My Acrylix® Stamp Set, Solos™ "P"
My Acrylix® Stamp Set, Sketchy Lowercase
Abundance Paper Packet
Abundance My Stickease™ Assortment
Chocolate Cardstock
Bamboo Cardstock
Brown Bag Exclusive Inks™ Pad
Chocolate Exclusive Inks™ Pad
Pewter My Accents™ Accessory Kit
Garden Green My Accents™ Accessory Kit
Designer Ribbon Rounds™ Cocoa Collection
Organdy Ribbon Rounds™ Basic Collection
Ribbon Rounds™ White Daisy Collection
Vellum
White Hemp
Bigger Brads Basic Collection
Pewter Eyelets
Photo Hangers
Hinges
Photo Clips
12" × 12" Pocket Photo Storage Pages
Pumpkin Seeds

## MEMOIRS COMPLETE (page 66)

*Technique: Journaling Decoration*

Accent your handwritten or printed journaling by drawing boxes or doodles around key words and using coloring pencils to shade and decorate. Using textured cardstock will give your doodles added appeal.

*Recipe*

My Acrylix® Stamp Set, Sans Small Lowercase
My Acrylix® Stamp Set, Calendar
My Acrylix® Stamp Set, Solos™ "C"
My Acrylix® Stamp Set, Solos™ "H"
My Acrylix® Stamp Set, Solos™ "R"
My Acrylix® Stamp Set, Solos™ "I"
My Acrylix® Stamp Set, Solos™ "S"
My Acrylix® Stamp Set, Solos™ "T"
My Acrylix® Stamp Set, Solos™ "M"
My Acrylix® Stamp Set, Solos™ "A"
Deck the Halls Paper Packet
Deck the Halls My Stickease™ Assortment
White Daisy Textured Cardstock
Black Exclusive Inks™ Pad
Dutch Blue Exclusive Inks™ Pad
Cranberry Exclusive Inks™ Marker
My Legacy Writer® Black Pen Set
Cranberry My Accents™ Accessory Kit
Designer Ribbon Rounds™ Cranberry Collection
Organdy Ribbon Rounds™ Summer Celebration Collection
Bigger Brads Basic Collection
Bigger Brads Winter Classic Collection
Coluzzle® File Folder
Dimensional Elements Basic Shapes
Photo Clips
Hinges
Photo Hangers
Liquid Glass
Coluzzle® Swivel Knife
Coluzzle® Cutting Mat
Watercolor Pencils
Thread
Paint

## CLASSICAL LOOK (page 68)

*Recipe*

My Acrylix® Stamp Set, Rustic Alphabet
My Acrylix® Stamp Set, Vintage Father's Day
My Acrylix® Stamp Set, El Fresco Phrases
My Acrylix® Stamp Set, Solos™ "M"
Simple Pleasures Paper Packet
Textured Cardstock Winter Cozy Combo
Desert Sand Exclusive Inks™ Pad
Cocoa Exclusive Inks™ Pad
VersaMark® Ink Pad
Silver Pearl Embossing Powder
Pewter My Accents™ Accessory Kit
Dimensional Elements Bookplates
Coluzzle® File Folder
Natural Hemp
Photo Clips
Hinges
Craft Heater
Round Sponge
¼" Long Reach Punch

## FOLLOW THE LEAD (page 70)

*Technique: Decorative Stitching*

Stitching on your pages is simple. Use your sewing machine for precise, even stitches or use your piercing tool to create a design and use a needle and thread to hand-stitch the details.

*Recipe*

My Acrylix® Stamp Set, Sans Small Caps
My Acrylix® Stamp Set, Sans Small Lowercase
My Acrylix® Stamp Set, Sans Small Numbers
My Acrylix® Stamp Set, Vroom Caps
My Acrylix® Stamp Set, Vroom Numbers
My Acrylix® Stamp Set, Solos™ "H"
My Acrylix® Stamp Set, Solos™ "A"
My Acrylix® Stamp Set, Solos™ "N"
My Acrylix® Stamp Set, Solos™ "O"
My Acrylix® Stamp Set, Solos™ "L"
My Acrylix® Stamp Set, Solos™ "Y"
My Acrylix® Stamp Set, Calendar
My Acrylix® Stamp Set, Rustic Alphabet
Crystal Blue Cardstock
Hollyhock Cardstock
Black Cardstock
Background and Texture Days To Cherish Combo Pack
Hollyhock Exclusive Inks™ Pad

Crystal Blue Exclusive Inks™ Pad
StazOn® Ink Pad
Dimensional Elements Basic Shapes
Hollyhock My Accents™ Accessory Kit
Black My Accents™ Accessory Kit
Designer Ribbon Rounds™ Hollyhock Collection
Window Charms™ Adhesive Squares
Black Embossing Powder
Tinted Embossing Pad
Black Waxy Flax
Liquid Glass
Hinges
Craft Heater
Sponge Daubers

## NICE & SIMPLE (page 72)

*Recipe*

My Acrylix® Stamp Set, Boutique Alphabet
My Acrylix® Stamp Set, A Friend Is…
Garden Green Cardstock
Olive Cardstock
Hollyhock Cardstock
Bamboo Cardstock
Cocoa Cardstock
Background and Texture Autumn Garden Combo Pack
Garden Green Exclusive Inks™ Pad
Olive Exclusive Inks™ Pad
Hollyhock Exclusive Inks™ Pad
Bamboo Exclusive Inks™ Pad
Cocoa Exclusive Inks™ Pad
StickStock™ Twill
Vellum
Designer Ribbon Rounds™ Cocoa Collection
Designer Ribbon Rounds™ Hollyhock Collection
Clear Inspirations™ Thank You Ribbon Slides
Clear Inspirations™ Believe Ribbon Slides
Pewter My Accents™ Accessory Kit
Garden Green My Accents™ Accessory Kit
Photo Hangers
Round Sponge
3-D Foam Squares
Thread

## SMALL PACKAGES (page 74)

*Technique: Holding Ribbon with Hinges*

Anchor your ribbon to the edge of your page by clipping a hinge over the end. Use a piercing tool to add holes to the ribbon and your paper. Insert two brads to secure.

*Recipe*

My Acrylix® Stamp Set, Calendar
My Acrylix® Stamp Set, Happy Birthday
Precious Paisleys Paper Packet
Hollyhock Exclusive Inks™ Pad
Pink Carnation Exclusive Inks™ Pad
White Daisy My Accents™ Accessory Kit
Dimensional Elements Ribbon Accents
Ribbon Rounds™ White Daisy Collection
Hinges
Thread

## FULL HOUSE (page 76)

*Recipe*

My Acrylix® Stamp Set, Solos™ "B"
My Acrylix® Stamp Set, Solos™ "O"
My Acrylix® Stamp Set, Solos™ "Y"
My Acrylix® Stamp Set, Solos™ "S"
Bamboo Cardstock
Olive Cardstock
Outdoor Denim Cardstock
Cranberry Cardstock
Colonial White Cardstock
Indian Corn Blue Cardstock
Indian Corn Blue Exclusive Inks™ Pad
Outdoor Denim Exclusive Inks™ Pad
My Legacy Writer® Black Pen Set
Dimensional Elements Bookplates
Sassy Strands™ Autumn Harvest Collection
Indian Corn Blue Eyelets
Outdoor Denim My Accents™ Accessory Kit
Photo Clips
Thread
Sandpaper

## SAFE & SECURE (page 78)

*Technique: Scissor Distressing*

Take the open or closed edge of your Micro-Tip scissors and rub perpendicularly along the edge of your cardstock. This is a fun way to distress the fibers of the paper and add texture to paper pieces or the edges of a page. Scissor distressing will especially stand out when using a cardstock with a white core. The result will be a piece that has a fine, white border.

*Recipe*

My Acrylix® Stamp Set, Calendar
My Acrylix® Stamp Set, Vroom Caps
My Acrylix® Stamp Set, Vroom Numbers
My Acrylix® Stamp Set, Sans Small Caps
Floral Impressions Paper Pack
Textured Cardstock Winter Cozy Combo Pack
White Daisy Textured Cardstock
Garden Green Exclusive Inks™ Pad
Grey Wool Exclusive Inks™ Pad
Ribbon Rounds™ White Daisy Collection
Dimensional Elements Ribbon Accents
Photo Clips
Bigger Brads Basic Collection
Photo Hangers
Sponge Daubers
Pewter Eyelets
Thread

## RHAPSODY (page 80)

*Recipe*

My Acrylix® Stamp Set, Outdoor Thoughts
My Acrylix® Stamp Set, Rustic Alphabet
My Acrylix® Stamp Set, Playful Lowercase
Background and Texture Autumn Harvest Combo Pack
Brown Bag Cardstock
Bamboo Cardstock
White Daisy Cardstock
Crystal Blue Cardstock
Bamboo Exclusive Inks™ Pad
Olive Exclusive Inks™ Pad
Brown Bag Exclusive Inks™ Pad
Indian Corn Blue Exclusive Inks™ Pad
Heavenly Blue Exclusive Inks™ Pad
Paper Circle Tags
Colonial White Waxy Flax
Silver My Accents™ Accessory Kit
Heavenly Blue Eyelets

Silver Brads
Decorative Wire
Photo Hangers
Sandpaper

## BITS & PIECES (page 82)

*Technique: Direct-to-Paper*

Apply ink to cardstock pieces by running the ink pad along the edges and corners, liberally or sparingly, as desired.

*Recipe*

My Acrylix® Stamp Set, Small Pleasures
Groovy Blossoms Paper Packet
Groovy Blossoms My Stickease™ Assortment
Cocoa Exclusive Inks™ Pad
Designer Ribbon Rounds™ Cocoa Collection
Garden Green My Accents™ Accessory Kit
Hollyhock My Accents™ Accessory Kit
White Daisy My Accents™ Accessory Kit
Bigger Brads Basic Collection
Thread

## BALANCED RHYTHM (page 84)

*Recipe*

My Acrylix® Stamp Set, Fluttering Frames
My Acrylix® Stamp Set, Boing! Alphabet
My Reflections Collection™ Graduation Kit
Cocoa Cardstock
Bamboo Cardstock
Colonial White Cardstock
Cocoa Exclusive Inks™ Pad
Clear Detail Embossing Powder
My Legacy Writer® Black Pen Set
Pewter My Accents™ Accessory Kit
Designer Ribbon Rounds™ Cocoa Collection
Dimensional Elements Ribbon Accents
Thread

## STACCATO (page 88)

*Technique: Journal Embellishments*

Put a fun twist on your journaling by formatting it into strips. Place a photo hanger underneath one end of the journaling. Loop a ribbon through the end. Pierce the ribbon with a piercing tool and add a brad.

*Recipe*

My Acrylix® Stamp Set, Calendar
Key Lime Cardstock
Carnation Cardstock
Hollyhock Cardstock
Olive Cardstock
Black Cardstock
White Daisy Cardstock
Hollyhock Exclusive Inks™ Pad
Dimensional Elements Ribbon Accents
Black Waxy Flax
Designer Ribbon Rounds™ Hollyhock Collection
Photo Hangers
Photo Clips
White Acrylic Paint
Thread

## PERSONALITY PRESENCE (page 90)

*Recipe*

My Acrylix® Stamp Set, Elegant Script
My Acrylix® Stamp Set, Vroom Caps
My Acrylix® Stamp Set, San Small Lowercase
My Acrylix® Stamp Set, Calendar
Days to Cherish Background and Texture Combo Pack
White Daisy Textured Cardstock
Bamboo Cardstock
Topiary Cardstock
Cranberry Cardstock
Desert Sand Cardstock
Topiary Exclusive Inks™ Pad
Cranberry Exclusive Inks™ Pad
Cocoa Exclusive Inks™ Pad
Bamboo Exclusive Inks™ Pad
Pewter My Accents™ Accessory Kit
Dimensional Elements Basic Shapes
Natural Hemp
Pewter Eyelets
Photo Clips
Thread

## STARS ABOVE (page 92)

*Technique: Faux Metal*

Combine Brilliance™ Metallic ink and Chocolate ink to create a faux metal look on cardstock. Apply the gold metallic ink directly to Bamboo cardstock, then sponge on Chocolate ink for shading.

*Recipe*

My Acrylix® Stamp Set, Bottle Caps
My Acrylix® Stamp Set, Sans Small Caps
My Acrylix® Stamp Set, Solos™ "E"
My Acrylix® Stamp Set, Vroom Caps
Cocoa Cardstock
Bamboo Cardstock
Barn Red Cardstock
Barn Red Exclusive Inks™ Pad
Cocoa Exclusive Inks™ Pad
Galaxy Gold Brilliance™ Metallic Ink Pad
Dimensional Elements Classic Alphabet
Dimensional Elements Basic Shapes
Pewter My Accents™ Accessory Kit
Bigger Brads Basic Collection
Natural Hemp
Large Dry Embossing Stylus

## SUBTITLES (page 94)

*Recipe*

My Acrylix® Stamp Set, Rustic Alphabet
My Acrylix® Stamp Set, Storytime Numbers
My Acrylix® Stamp Set, Top Secret
Background and Texture Spring Harmony Combo Pack
Bamboo Cardstock
Crystal Blue Cardstock
White Daisy Cardstock
Cocoa Cardstock
Chocolate Exclusive Inks™ Pad
Cocoa Exclusive Inks™ Pad
Dimensional Elements Bookplates
Dimensional Elements Basic Shapes
Natural Hemp
Paper Circle Tags
Colonial White Waxy Flax
Hinges
Pewter Eyelets
Burlap
Brown Button
Paint
Beads
Sand & Shells
Antiqued Brads

## OPEN FORUM (page 96)

*Technique: Denting Oversized Brads*

Complete an accent with an oversized brad and then gently hammer the eyelet setter into the center of the brad to dent the surface.

*Recipe*

My Acrylix® Stamp Set, A Little Something
My Acrylix® Stamp Set, The Simple Things
My Acrylix® Stamp Set, Solos™ "B"
My Acrylix® Stamp Set, Solos™ "F"
Watermelon Cardstock
White Daisy Cardstock
Kiwi Cardstock
Bubblegum Cardstock
Background and Texture Spring Blosssom Combo Pack
Background and Texture Summer Celebration Combo Pack
Watermelon Exclusive Inks™ Pad
Black Exclusive Inks™ Pad
Kiwi Exclusive Inks™ Pad
Bubblegum Exclusive Inks™ Pad
Just Blooms™ Autumn Daisy Paper Flowers
Bigger Brads Basic Collection
Write 'n Rub™ Pen
Prisma Glitter
Dimensional Elements Basic Shapes
Sassy Strands™ White Daisy Collection
Sponge Daubers
Small Embossing Stylus
Paper Crimper

## SUPPORTING CAST (page 98)

*Recipe*

My Acrylix® Stamp Set, School Zone
My Acrylix® Stamp Set, Sans Small Caps
My Acrylix® Stamp Set, Sans Small Lowercase
School Zone Paper Packet
White Daisy Cardstock
Cranberry Exclusive Inks™ Pad
White Embossing Powder
Vellum StickStock™
Cranberry Eyelets
Cranberry Waxy Flax
Dimensional Elements Classic Alphabet
Dimensional Elements Basic Shapes
Dimensional Elements Bookplates
Cranberry My Accents™ Accessory Kit
Liquid Glass

## THUMBNAILS (page 100)

*Technique: Stamping on Metal*

To stamp on metal, choose a fast-drying solvent ink, such as StazOn® ink. Stamp a coordinating image with the ink directly to metal accents for added detail. Wait 3–5 minutes for the ink to dry.

*Recipe*

My Acrylix® Stamp Set, Romantic Backgrounds
Heirloom Paper Packet
Bamboo Cardstock
Desert Sand Exclusive Inks™ Pad
Bamboo Exclusive Inks™ Pad
StazOn® Ink Pad
Pewter My Accents™ Accessory Kit
Dimensional Elements Ribbon Accents
Organdy Ribbon Rounds™ Basic Collection
Photo Clips
Sponge Daubers
Round Sponge

## DOUBLE TAKE (page 102)

*Recipe*

My Acrylix® Stamp Set, Precious Alphabet
My Acrylix® Stamp Set, Classic Caps
My Acrylix® Stamp Set, Calendar
My Acrylix® Stamp Set, Retro Flowers
My Acrylix® Stamp Set, Beautifully Spring
My Acrylix® Stamp Set, Happy Easter
My Acrylix® Stamp Set, Egg.Cited
Colonial White Cardstock
Pink Carnation Cardstock
Buttercup Cardstock
Baby Pink Exclusive Inks™ Pad
Buttercup Exclusive Inks™ Pad
Pink Carnation Exclusive Inks™ Pad
White Daisy Exclusive Inks™ Pad
Colonial White My Accents™ Accessory Kit
Just Blooms™ Autumn Daisy Paper Flowers
Sponge Daubers

## CREATIVE TEAM (page 104)

*Technique: Letters in Relief*

Decorate the negative space of any chipboard letter block. Add a back to the letter block and fill the letter space with glitter, Fun Flock, or any fine accent.

*Recipe*

My Acrylix® Stamp Set, Giggle Caps
My Acrylix® Stamp Set, Giggle Lowercase
Heavenly Blue Cardstock
Crystal Blue Cardstock
Grey Wool Cardstock
Black Cardstock
White Daisy Textured Cardstock
True Black Archival Exclusive Inks™ Pad
Crystal Blue Exclusive Inks™ Pad
Heavenly Blue Exclusive Inks™ Pad
Vellum
Sassy Strands™ White Daisy Collection
Silver My Accents™ Accessory Kit
Glitter Stack
Rubber Brayer
Photo Hangers
Sponge Daubers
Pencil
Cutting Knife

## ROLE PLAY (page 106)

*Recipe*

My Acrylix® Stamp Set, Rustic Alphabet
My Acrylix® Stamp Set, Vroom Caps
My Acrylix® Stamp Set, Precious Alphabet
More to Adore Paper Packet
More to Adore My Stickease™ Assortment
Colonial White Cardstock
Chocolate Cardstock
Hollyhock Cardstock
Chocolate Exclusive Inks™ Pad
Colonial White Waxy Flax
Corner Rounder
Empressor® Guide
Empressing Tool
3-D Foam Squares

## GRAND FINALE (page 108)

*Technique: Layering-Cutouts*

Stamp a flower image on multiple colors of cardstock and B&T papers several times. Trim individual petals and arrange to create a dimensional accent. For larger flowers, begin by placing petals in the desired size and shape. Build inward, gluing layers of petals until the ends of the petals meet in the center. Add a smaller flower or a punched circle to the top for a nice center. Secure with a brad or eyelet.

*Recipe*

My Acrylix® Stamp Set, Because I Love You
My Acrylix® Stamp Set, Rustic Flowers
Sonata Paper Packet
Colonial White Cardstock
Blush Cardstock
Spring Iris Cardstock
Lilac Mist Cardstock
Blush Exclusive Inks™ Pad
Butterfly Exclusive Inks™ Pad
Spring Iris Exclusive Inks™ Pad
Lilac Mist Exclusive Inks™ Pad
Vanilla Cream Exclusive Inks™ Pad
Colonial White Exclusive Inks™ Pad
My Legacy Writer® Black Pen Set
White Daisy Eyelets
Coluzzle® Hula Uppercase
Round Sponge
Thread

## UNDERSTUDY (page 110)

*Recipe*

My Acrylix® Stamp Set, Solos™ "M"
My Acrylix® Stamp Set, Solos™ "A"
My Acrylix® Stamp Set, Solos™ "K"
My Acrylix® Stamp Set, Solos™ "S"
My Acrylix® Stamp Set, Sans Small Lowercase
My Acrylix® Stamp Set, Sans Small Numbers
My Acrylix® Stamp Set, Giggle Lowercase
My Acrylix® Stamp Set, Calendar
Cranberry Cardstock
Star Spangled Blue Cardstock
Cranberry Exclusive Inks™ Pad
Bamboo Exclusive Inks™ Pad
Star Spangled Blue Exclusive Inks™ Pad
Days to Cherish Background and Texture Combo Pack
White Daisy Textured Cardstock
VersaMark® Ink Pad
Clear Detail Embossing Powder
Cranberry My Accents™ Accessory Kit
White Daisy My Accents™ Accessory Kit
Designer Ribbon Rounds™ Cranberry Collection
Moonstruck Waxy Flax
Colonial White Waxy Flax
Dimensional Elements Ribbon Accents
Photo Hangers
Star Spangled Blue Eyelets
Round Sponge
Craft Heater
Thread
Paint

## SWING RHYTHM (page 112)

*Technique: Stamp Shading*

Stamp an image in a medium tone (on lighter paper) and then use a Sponge Dauber to add depth. Shade the outside of the image with a darker ink and the inside with a lighter ink. Crinkle the paper and trim carefully.

*Recipe*

My Acrylix® Stamp Set, Autumn Splendor
My Acrylix® Stamp Set, Classic Caps
My Acrylix® Stamp Set, Calendar
Desert Sand Cardstock

Bamboo Cardstock
Textured Cardstock Autumn Harvest Combo Pack
Days to Cherish Background and Texture Combo Pack
Desert Sand Exclusive Inks™ Pad
Garnet Exclusive Inks™ Pad
Bamboo Exclusive Inks™ Pad
Autumn Terracotta Exclusive Inks™ Pad
Photo Clips
Pewter My Accents™ Accessory Kit
Natural Hemp
Dimensional Elements Ribbon Accents
Dimensional Elements Bookplates
Sponge Daubers
Round Sponge
Sandpaper

## SHADOW (page 114)

*Recipe*

My Acrylix® Stamp Set, Boutique Alphabet
My Acrylix® Stamp Set, Sans Small Caps
My Acrylix® Stamp Set, Calendar
Snips & Snails Paper Packet
Bamboo Cardstock
Baby Pink Cardstock
White Daisy Textured Cardstock
Bamboo Exclusive Inks™ Pad
Heavenly Blue Exclusive Inks™ Pad
Colonial White My Accents™ Accessory Kit
Baby Pink My Accents™ Accessory Kit
Buttercup My Accents™ Accessory Kit
Heavenly Blue My Accents™ Accessory Kit
Sassy Strands™ White Daisy Collection
Just Blooms™ Autumn Daisy Paper Flowers
Indian Corn Blue Waxy Flax
Liquid Glass
Metal Circle Tags
Bigger Brads Spring Harmony Collection
Bigger Brads Winter Classic Collection
Round Sponge
Thread
Paint
Sandpaper

## OVERTURE (page 116)

*Technique: Clear Embossing Titles*

Cover chipboard Dimensional Elements with cardstock. Rub an embossing ink pad onto the covered letters, then sprinkle with clear embossing powder. Use an embossing heat tool to heat the powder to a shiny finish. This will add subtle, yet noticeable detail to any colored cardstock.

*Recipe*

My Acrylix® Stamp Set, Sans Small Caps
Vintage Travel Paper Packet
Colonial White Cardstock
Indian Corn Blue Cardstock
Cocoa Exclusive Inks™ Pad
Dimensional Elements Bookplates
Dimensional Elements Classic Alphabet
Designer Ribbon Rounds™ Twilight Collection
Colonial White My Accents™ Accessory Kit
Chocolate Waxy Flax
Colonial White Waxy Flax
Photo Clips
Photo Hangers
Hinges

## SALSA (page 118)

*Recipe*

My Acrylix® Stamp Set, Air Mail
Vintage Travel Paper Packet
Outdoor Denim Cardstock
Cocoa Exclusive Inks™ Pad
Ribbon Rounds™ White Daisy Collection
Pewter My Accents™ Accessory Kit
Photo Clips
Photo Hangers
Hinges
Natural Hemp
Round Sponge